No!

No!

A Theological Response to Christian Reconstructionism

PAUL C. MCGLASSON

CASCADE *Books* · Eugene, Oregon

NO!

A Theological Response to Christian Reconstructionism

Cascade Books
An Imprint of Wipf and Stock Publishers
199 W. 8th Ave., Suite 3
Eugene, OR 97401

www.wipfandstock.com

ISBN 13: 978-1-61097-867-5

Cataloging-in-Publication data:

McGlasson, Paul C.

No! : a theological response to Christian reconstructionism / Paul C. McGlasson.

viii + 134 p. ; 23 cm. —Includes bibliographical references

ISBN 13: 978-1-61097-867-5

1. Evangelicalism—United States—Controversial literature. 2. Conservatism—Religious aspects. 3. United States—Church history—20th Century. I. Title.

BR1642.U5 M29 2012

Manufactured in the U.S.A.

"There has been a change in the weather. I had almost relaxed and thought the matter was finished; but then it suddenly arises anew . . ."

Martin Luther
Against the Heavenly Prophets (1525)

Contents

Acknowledgments

I WOULD LIKE TO EXPRESS my deep gratitude to Rodney Clapp for his excellent work as editor of this volume; to my wife Peggy, who read each chapter as it was written, and returned it with invaluable constructive criticism; to the staff of Wipf and Stock / Cascade Books, for their rare and pleasant combination of rigorous professionalism and friendly congeniality; and to the congregation I serve, who are to me a daily reminder of the true meaning of the gospel.

Introduction

EVERYWHERE, IT SEEMS, ONE hears talk: "Wasn't our country founded as a Christian nation? Shouldn't we vote only for Christian candidates, willing to stand up for our beliefs? After all, isn't the Christian worldview the exact opposite of our modern secular society; why should Christians sit back and do nothing?" The talk often grows in intensity: "And what about our public schools? If we don't teach our children basic Christian values, what will happen to our society then? Why shouldn't we teach the Ten Commandments like we used to; after all, our nation was founded on biblical principles! Why do Christians have to accept the modernist relativism all around us; why shouldn't we fight back, and do something!"

The talk has arguably grown in volume in recent years. It takes place in Sunday school classes, where earnest Christians endeavor to discern God's will for church and society; it takes place in conversations between fellow Christians, simply trying to sort out the issues of our time; it takes place on talk radio, where it often shapes the debating points of the day; it takes place in political speeches, where various candidates use such talk for their campaign agenda. The volume occasionally dies down, only to rise again; for some reason, the talk does not seem to go away. For better or worse, it is simply there, humming away in the background and oftentimes the foreground of modern religious-political life.

The talk is simply there; but *behind* the talk is a religious movement known as Christian Reconstructionism, also known as theonomy, or dominion theology. The purpose of the present essay is straightforward. It aims to offer an explanation of Christian Reconstructionism, and a theological response to it.

Christian Reconstructionism can be looked at in two different ways. On the one hand, it can be studied as a religious movement which has developed over the last half century within the ranks of conservative evangelicalism. Such a study would involve names and dates; the inter-relationship of various figures and institutions; in essence, the stuff of history and sociology.

The fact is, there are already several good books quite useful for this purpose. I would highly recommend three in particular. *Fundamentalism and American Culture,* by George Marsden, is an epic and brilliant history of American fundamentalism from the turn of the century to the present. Here, Christian Reconstructionism as a religious movement will be seen in the widest context possible. Narrowing the historical context a bit—but certainly not the quality of scholarship—is *Roads to Dominion,* by Sara Diamond. Here, the story begins in the post-War period, and shows a sociologist's eye for broader institutional context. Finally, there is *Redeeming America,* by Michael Lienesch. Here the scope is narrowest of all, focusing exclusively on the New Religious Right beginning in the 1980s, with the added benefit of detail the narrower scope allows. Any and all of these books can be read with confidence and great profit.

As a religious movement, there is certainly little doubt concerning the influence of Christian Reconstructionism, which is evidently growing. Two examples must here suffice. Most will remember that Governor Rick Perry of Texas launched his bid for the Republican nomination for President of the United States with a prayer rally in Houston, Texas, in August of 2011. Called "The Response," the rally was designed as a Christians-only effort to call on divine support for Perry's candidacy, as well as to "claim" the United States for a new Christian religious transformation in the political realm. The rally was largely organized and supported by a group known as the New Apostolic Reformation, led by C. Peter Wagner, a former long-time faculty member at Fuller Seminary. The point is simply this: The New Apostolic Reformation is in fact a branch of Christian Reconstructionism. Put simply, Christian Reconstructionsim, as a religious movement, was there to launch a major campaign for the presidency of the United States.

The second example is less overt, but in its own way perhaps far more influential in the long run. In his standard account, *Homeschool: An American History*, Milton Gaither lists among the three pioneers of the modern homeschooling movement Rousas J. Rushdoony (whom we will meet again below as a major figure in Christian Reconstructionism). According to Gaither, the influence of Rushdoony on the entire Christian homeschooling movement has been "direct and powerful."[1] In its search for what it considers an authentically Christian curriculum, the various homeschooling communities (and for that matter many independent Christian schools as well) have found in the writings of Rushdoony exactly the sort of vigorous account of a truly Christian society desired. Textbooks, organizations, and popular individual authors, all heavily influenced by Rushdoony, "took control of the homeschooling movement, giving it a distinctively dominionist flavor."[2] Consequently, the explosive growth of the Christian homeschool movement in part accounts for the outsized spread of Christian Reconstructionism.

But there is another way of looking at Christian Reconstructionism: not simply as a religious movement, but as a theological *set of ideas*. It is as a *set of ideas* that I propose to consider Christian Reconstructionism in this book. For the fact is, the *set of ideas* spawned by the movement have now passed over into the general religious-political lexicon of our time. People who are not Christian Reconstructionists, people who perhaps have never even heard of Christian Reconstructionism, are nevertheless using these ideas in their talk (some have called this phenomenon "soft Reconstructionism"). The time is surely ripe therefore for a careful theological examination of the *set of ideas* which make up Christian Reconstructionism, especially for those who hear the talk and for one reason or another want to know further what it all means.

My examination of the set of ideas of Christian Reconstructionism will proceed in two parts. First of all, I will do my best to present as objectively as possible the ideas as they are contained in the primary writings of the major proponents of the movement. And then I will offer a serious theological critique of this set of ideas, in which I argue that Christian Reconstruction falls well outside the boundary of mainstream, historic, orthodox Christianity. That is to say, I will make the case that Christian Reconstructionism is a serious distortion of the gospel, highly misleading in its depiction of the core of biblical truth; and therefore the ecumenical church at large should reject it as false doctrine.

Let me stress firmly at the outset: I will be arguing against ideas, *theological positions*, not people. God alone knows the human heart; who are we to judge? Nevertheless, there is no point arguing over a position

1. Gaither, *Homeschool*, 137.
2. Ibid., 147.

unless it is being accurately represented; surely the reader expects nothing less. So, in the first part, when expounding the primary ideas of Christian Reconstructionsim, I will draw those ideas from representative books, and will endeavor fairly and accurately to represent those ideas, before offering the critical response in the second. I suggest that there are four central ideas that constitute the core of Christian Reconstructionism: epistemological dualism, the direct application of mosaic law in society, cultural Christianity, and Christian political domination. A quick survey of these four ideas will help to get a sense of the whole, before we elaborate upon them in detail in the chapters that follow.

By the first central idea, *epistemological dualism*, is meant the notion that Scripture is self-asserting in such a way that only those who already presuppose its truth can understand it. There can therefore be absolutely no common ground whatsoever between Christian and non-Christian, believer and non-believer, the church and the world. According to this position, even well-established theologians of the past have failed to recognize this crucial dividing line—a line drawn and maintained by God himself—between believers and non-believers. Epistemological dualism holds that no connecting link can ever cross over this yawning chasm: whether philosophical, scientific, or any form of consensus-building or coalition. I shall expound upon these ideas and explain them further, as they are contained in the well-known apologetic treatise of Cornelius Van Til, *A Christian Theory of Knowledge*.

The second idea—the direct application of *mosaic law in society*—will be presented on the basis of the comprehensive book of Rousas John Rushdoony, *The Institutes of Biblical Law*. According to Rushdoony, the laws of Moses contained in the Pentateuch operate in the form of abstract legal and moral principles. These legal and moral principles can be, and should be, applied to contemporary society in the form of biblical case law. In other words, this mosaic system of "principles and cases" drawn from the Old Testament should in fact provide the basis of the legal system, not only for Christians, but for all peoples. We will want to look at Rushdoony's understanding of biblical "case law" more closely; and to flesh it out, examine some of the examples derived from his legal system, such as the death penalty for a variety of "sexual sins."

The third idea of *cultural Christianity* holds that genuine Christian spirituality operates with a logic of totals. To believe in the Truth of the Bible means to have an all-embracing, all-encompassing worldview—in

fact, to create a Christian culture. This Christian culture should ide-
ally operate everywhere: in government, in schools, in families, in every
sector of society. It is said that it once did—back in the "early days of
America"—but it is now in a life or death struggle with its deadly opponent, secular humanism. These two worldviews—the Christian and
the secular humanist—are exact opposites in every way, and cannot live
side by side. One must win, the other must lose. The goal of Christians
must be to insure—even under extraordinary measures of applied
force—the complete victory of the Christian worldview in the totality of society. The best-selling work by Francis Schaeffer, *A Christian
Manifesto*, will provide us with an opportunity to examine this concept
of cultural Christianity in detail.

Fourth—and in a sense gathering up all previous points into the
final important point—is the notion of *Christian political domination*, as
expounded in *Christian Reconstructionism: What It Is, What It Isn't*, by
Gary North and Gary DeMar. Given the twofold division of humanity into
believer and non-believer; given the proper role of mosaic law in supply-
ing the legal system of society; given the cultural mandate of Christians
to shape all reality; what should Christians now be doing? The authors
argue that "comprehensive evangelism" is the answer, which means nothing less than "socio-political domination of the world" by Christians. God
has given Christians the task of winning absolute dominion in the world,
by establishing a Christian civilization; and political power through confrontation, not consensus, is the means to accomplish it. The secular state
must go, for it is the realm of Satan.

I will in a moment outline in brief the fourfold theological response
to Christian Reconstructionism I will offer in part 2; but first I think it
helpful to make very clear at the outset the basis, nature, and sources of
my response. I am a confessing Christian; and I will respond theologically
on the basis of the church's confession of the risen Christ as sole Lord and
Savior of all creation. The confessing heritage of the church is now sadly
fragmented into Protestant, Roman Catholic, and Eastern Orthodox
forms; nevertheless, I believe in the one universal reality of the church
embracing all Christians, a reality which is founded upon the one gospel
of Jesus Christ attested in Holy Scripture. The true content of Christian
confession, however, is not a given; it has to be sought again and again in
each new age of the church. One purpose of this essay is simply to ask:
what does scripturally-based orthodox Christianity today have to say in

the light of these ideas coming from the movement known as Christian Reconstructionism? For the fact is, Christians of all communions now struggle with these issues.

The nature of that question itself needs further explanation. The first article of Christian confession in the early church was to receive and adopt the Scriptures of the Old and New Testament as canon. That basic decision is far-reaching in its consequences; for it defines the arena in which God's Word is to be sought, in which God's will for church and society is to be discerned by the faithful for all time.

Now, the authority of Scripture as canon cuts two different ways. On the one hand, the canon of Scripture embraces legitimate theological diversity within the one church of Christ. Even though there is only one gospel, it comes to us refracted through the very different witnesses of Matthew, Mark, Luke, and John. Diversity of theological opinion— say between Lutherans and Reformed, or between East and West—is legitimated by the church's confession of canon. On the other hand, canon establishes boundaries, outside of which the gospel is not rightly discerned and affirmed. While the fourfold gospel is left in its diverse witness, the gnostic Gospel of Thomas is excluded. By its very nature canon sets limits; it defines theological positions outside those limits, not as legitimate diversity, but as serious and fundamental distortion of the truth of the gospel.

The theological response I am offering here to Christian Reconstructionism is a serious one. I am convinced that it is not a question of legitimate theological diversity, one Christian movement among others in the larger body of Christ, like Methodists and Baptists. Rather, it is a serious and fundamental distortion of the gospel, which is leading people further away rather than closer to the central affirmation of Christian witness.

I will call on three different sources to substantiate and elucidate this theological response in part 2 of this work. First, I will refer at times to the creeds and confessions of the church: those moments where the church has gathered to confess the faith against false doctrine. Does Christian Reconstructionism embrace the truth of the gospel as contained in the creeds and confessions of the church? Second, I will also draw upon several of the great theologians of the past, especially the church fathers (east and west), and the Protestant Reformers. I am not suggesting that new insight is no longer possible in the church, far from it; but I do suggest that a form of teaching completely different *in kind* from all that has gone before in the mainstream of historic Christianity casts serious doubts upon itself. Third, and by far the most important, I will look directly at Holy Scripture itself, examining by theological exegesis of Scripture the key points at issue. When the gospel is at stake, the church always takes its stand ultimately upon Holy Scripture as the Word of God.

The confession of Holy Scripture as canon—as the normative authority of faith and practice in the church of Jesus Christ—draws together the theological strengths of all major communions: Roman Catholic, Eastern Orthodox, and Protestant. Scripture is received in the church as a living witness to the risen Lord Jesus Christ, whose authority over all things is the one true content of the Bible, and the one genuine measure of its truth. The content of the Bible has a coherent shape, a pattern of truth; the early church called it the rule of faith, the Reformers called it the analogy of faith. The pattern of truth in the Bible is not a system of logically derived propositions; it is ultimately Jesus Christ himself, present by his Spirit to teach and instruct the faith in "sound doctrine" (1 Tim. 4:6). Sound doctrine does not mean *same* doctrine; there is legitimate room for disagreement within the context of canon. But commitment to sound doctrine in the church does mean a willingness to say no to unsound, unwholesome, false doctrine.

And that the church has done on occasion throughout its history— reluctantly but decisively—when circumstances necessitate such a response. For example, in the early church, a movement known as Arianism became sufficiently widespread as to call forth such a response; for it taught that Jesus is crucial for faith, but not fully divine. Against the Arian party, the Nicene Creed responds theologically on the basis of Scripture that Jesus Christ is in fact fully divine—of the same substance with the Father—as well as paradoxically fully human. Or again, in the twentieth century, a party known as the German Christians attempted to wed the gospel to a political ideology, the fascism of Adolf Hitler. In the Barmen Declaration of 1934, the confessing church responded theologically by declaring that Jesus Christ alone is God's Word to humanity, and must not be fused with a political force arising from the old world of sin. In these and other cases, the gathered church, on the basis of Scripture as canon, was not saying: we disagree with our opponents, but of course must learn to agree to disagree. That happens, and should happen in many, many, cases, but not these. Rather, they gathered to say: this is not the sound doctrine we find in Holy Scripture as God's Word, and should not be seen as a legitimate expression of what we teach and how we live in the community of faith in the risen Lord.

I am convinced that Christian Reconstructionism departs in its essentials—not just in peripheral details—from the pattern of sound doctrine in Scripture. In part 2 I will offer four responses to each of the points in part 1.

In response to the notion of *epistemological dualism*, I will argue that the cross of Jesus Christ according to Scripture radically eliminates all thinking in terms of "us" vs. "them." The narrative of the crucifixion in the canonical gospels draws a line, but it is not a line between the friends and supporters of Jesus and his enemies. Rather, the disciples, the Romans, the Jews, indeed the whole world, is on one side of the line, and Jesus alone is on the other. Jesus goes to the cross alone, carrying the sins of the whole world, in order to redeem all humanity. The cross is therefore the end of all dividing walls between human beings, tearing down every barrier erected in the name of "religion." Against the epistemological dualism of Christian Reconstructionism therefore I will point to the church's ultimate commitment to the *open proclamation of the gospel to all people*.

In response to the notion of applying *mosaic law in society* in the form of abstract moral "principles and cases," I will call to mind the simple but profound fact that there are no abstract moral principles anywhere in the Bible, including the mosaic law of the Old Testament. God's Word does not come to humanity as abstract moral principles, according to Scripture; rather God speaks in specific, concrete commands: do this, go here, come, etc. In the Bible, there are no abstract principles standing between God and humanity, principles which of course can be easily manipulated. There is only the sheer sovereign reality of God who commands, and the concrete response of obedience. Nor is there any room for "case law" in the Bible, which is a human endeavor to make applications based on "moral cases." The biblical word does not work that way. Rather, the only source of the knowledge of God's will is his active, living communication; and the only response is to do it. And finally, we will point to classic theologians in the early church and the Reformation who unanimously reject the idea that the ceremonial and judicial laws of the Old Testament should become the contemporary law of nations. The issue at stake is the fundamental relation of *law and gospel*.

In response to the idea of a *cultural Christianity*, I will point to the radically new reality of the gospel, which turns the religious and moral values of this world upside down ("You have heard that it was said . . . but I say unto you . . ." (cf. Matt 5–7). The gospel is the breaking into reality of the utterly new world of God, which serves no personal, cultural, or national agenda whatsoever. Rather, God's new world reaches out to embrace all races, all tribes, all nations, all peoples of the earth. From the very beginning, the one mission of the church is a global commission: "You will be my witnesses . . . to the ends of the earth" (Acts 1:8). And with surprise and astonishment, this global mission of the church has become more a visible reality in the last few decades than at any other time in the church's life, as a result of the recent explosive growth of Christianity in the global community. The very time period when Christian Reconstructionism was narrowing the scope of the gospel to national self-renewal, the gospel itself was breaking through all boundaries to transform all nations and peoples in the light of the risen Christ. To seek to tie the gospel to the self-interests of any one nation—the whole notion of America as a "Christian nation"—whatever its historical merits, fundamentally distorts the *call to global mission* that constitutes the basic commission of the church.

In response to the notion of *Christian political domination* I will set our fundamental call to discipleship according to Scripture, which is to be conformed to the image of Christ. Just as Jesus did not come to be served, but to serve, so we are conformed to the image of Christ in outer service of others, especially the weak and the vulnerable. Whenever the church has tried to identify its own interests directly with the kingdom of God, it has experienced miserable failure—the medieval crusades come to mind. Just as the church rejects the notion of a totalitarian state, which dominates the voice and actions of all people, so the church rejects the notion of a totalitarian religion, which establishes the laws and dominates the conduct of society. Christ is Lord; not the church. The biblical *call to discipleship* is not a call to dominate the world, but explicitly and directly a call to serve Christ in word and deed.

Finally, in an epilogue to the book, our attention will turn, however briefly, to a new direction. If Christian Reconstructionism fails to offer orthodox ecumenical Christianity a satisfying, biblical and moral vision of the role of Christians in society, what is the alternative?

Reconstruction, by definition, looks backward, seeking to reconstruct what is believed to have been lost. The gospel, on the other hand, always draws us forward to God's new world, already established in the death and resurrection of Jesus Christ. In Christ, God has already transformed the whole of creation; what does it mean for Christians to live in the world in the light of that radiant divine transformation? On the basis of Scripture we will stress four points: first, the inherent value of democracy as a divine right for all peoples and nations; second, the need for economic equality, in a world which is becoming increasingly polarized between the wealthy and the poor; third, the embrace of the outsider, the foreigner, the marginalized in our global society; and finally, the relative value of human culture (including government, art, science, education, and so forth) for Christian existence under God's gracious care. All of these are joined together in a force more powerful than any false quest for dominion over the other, indeed the most powerful force in the world: the power of love. The Christian is to participate in nothing less than *a new society.*

CHAPTER 1

Epistemological Dualism

WE PROCEED NOW TO the first of our set of four concepts which define Christian Reconstructionism. We have called it *epistemological dualism*, and we propose to examine the book by Cornelius Van Til, *A Christian Theory of Knowledge*, in setting out this concept. It would of course be an obvious alternative to define at the outset what we mean by the rather cumbersome term epistemological dualism, and the reader rightly expects a clear definition—and will be given one in due course. However, I must ask the reader's patience. There seems to be little point in offering a definition of the phrase, and then applying it to Van Til; surely that does little more than show that Van Til's work can be bent to conform to my definition. Far more fruitful—and in the end far more convincing—would be to delay the definition until the matter is before us, and only then use the phrase to draw attention to the salient features of Van Til's view: features which make it such a powerful force in initiating the momentum of the Christian Reconstructionist movement.

The first question we need to address in approaching *A Christian Theory of Knowledge* is what genre of theological writing and research it belongs to. It is not biblical interpretation; though the book refers often to Scripture, it contains only a few references to actual verses of the Bible, and virtually no in-depth theological exegesis of Scripture. It is not dogmatic theology; while it often uses the word *God*, it again contains no sustained theological exposition of any of the great concepts or themes of Christian witness such as the Trinity, Christology, Creation, Grace, Faith, Justification, and so forth. It is certainly not homiletics; the book contains

11

no references whatsoever to the evangelical call to mission, or to the task of proclamation. So what is it?

Van Til himself calls it an exercise in "apologetics"; and while he is certainly content to leave it at that, I think a word or two of historical context would be helpful in interpreting the rest of the book. In one form or another, such fields as biblical interpretation, dogmatic theology, and homiletics have been part of the church's theological labor throughout its history; "apologetics" has not. To be sure, in the early church there were a group of writers known as the "Apologists," writers such as Justin Martyr, Aristides, Tatian, and Athenagoras. They wrote "apologies" of the faith at a time when Christianity was still a persecuted religion, and their aim was largely to convince legal authority and literate public alike that such persecution was unjust and unworthy. They saw their writing as a *positive* affirmation of the gospel mission, despite the extraordinary circumstances faced by these early Christians.

But *apologetics* is different in kind from these ad hoc early Christian efforts. For apologetics, as conceived by Van Til and many others, did not arise as a genre until well into the nineteenth century. Apologetics came, so to speak, on the other end of the historical parabola defining the relation of Christianity to the surrounding culture. The early church apologists wrote when Christianity was not yet accepted within the public forum; apologetics arose when Christianity was becoming marginalized by that same forum. With the coming of the Enlightenment in the eighteenth century, modern science, philosophy, economics, political philosophy, etc., were emerging as independent disciplines no longer looking to the church for primary validation or guidance. Modern humanity—so it was perceived—came into its own, standing on its own two feet without need for faith. Some Christian thinkers tried to respond to this situation by seeking to *defend* the gospel in the face of modern secular culture; and the defense offered is called apologetics, from the Greek word for defense. Hence, unlike the ad hoc efforts of the early church, the modern genre of apologetics is systematic, defensive in posture, critical, and largely at home in high culture debates rather than proclamation or the mission field.

Now, one option for modern apologetics is to assume some neutral ground between faith and unbelief, between believer and non-believer. On this view, if a believer looks at the world of nature and an unbeliever looks at the same world of nature, there will be observations and laws that both can see with equal clarity and agreement. Such observations and laws are simply "out there." Because of this neutral ground between belief and unbelief, the believer has the basis for a strategy of persuasion; the believer can use the neutral facts already admitted by the unbeliever as building blocks for an argument for the truths of Christian faith.

This strategy of persuasion was most famously used by the highly influential treatise by Joseph Butler, *The Analogy of Religion, Natural and Revealed, to the Constitution and Course of Nature* (1736). As Butler argued, "everything is what it is, and not another thing."[1] That is to say, a fact is a fact, whether a believer sees it, or a non-believer. This neutral ground of mere factuality allows for the enterprise of natural theology, which is the effort to show the unbeliever the marks of God in the natural world through natural reason. Butler continues: "All reasonable men know certainly, that there cannot, in reality, be any such thing as chance; and conclude, that things which have this appearance are the result of general laws, and may be reduced into them."[2] Surely everyone admits that natural laws govern the universe; given this universally reasonable assertion—the same for both believers and non-believers—a case for God can then be made. The Butler-inspired tradition of "facts and evidences" for Christianity has of course remained strong in some circles to this day.

Van Til continues to embrace wholeheartedly the genre of apologetics; he aims to give a biblically based defense of Christianity in the face of modern secular culture. However, he vigorously and systematically rejects the "facts and evidences" tradition of natural theology found in Butler and his many imitators. Let us now proceed to lay out the basics of Van Til's approach, and then follow by examining in some detail several elements of it.

According to Van Til, the main approach of Christian apologetics should be this: modern thought *as a whole* has a profound predicament which it cannot under any circumstances solve within the resources at its command. Modern thought in all its variety of manifestations—philosophy, art, science, indeed culture in general—operates with a set of principles which cannot under any circumstances be avoided. And those very principles condemn all modern thinkers, all modern cultural adherents, to a necessarily self-contradictory and self-destructive position.

1. Butler, *Analogy*, x.
2. Ibid., xi.

By contrast, Christianity has a set of principles that alone solve the self-contradictory quandary of all modern culture.

Basic to Van Til's position is that there is one and only one Christian way of thinking, "the Christian position,"[3] and he nowhere deviates from this sense that all Christianity on the one hand, and all modernity on the other can be encapsulated into a single set of rational propositions. All Christians reason one way; all non-Christians reason another way; it cannot possibly be any different. (Actually, we need to quality the first statement a bit, as we shall see in our further elaboration of his view. Not all Christians realize the right way to reason in a Christian way. Many Christians fail to grasp the proper method of following the biblical method of reasoning. But of this Van Til is certain; there is only one *biblical* method of reasoning, and it ought to be followed by all Christians even though sadly it is not.)

So, what is the Christian principle, the one biblical way of reasoning? The foundational principle of all Christian thought is that God is completely and utterly self-sufficient. He exists in himself alone, and for himself alone; and therefore he defines himself alone. God is a completely self-explanatory reality. That means that all human autonomy—all human independence in relation to God—must be radically excluded. It has to be either/or; either God is all and humanity nothing; or humanity is all and God nothing. Either humanity is completely dependent upon God, or God must be in some way dependent upon humanity. Now, if God is completely self-sufficient and completely self-explanatory, this has global implications for the way humanity knows reality. Every fact is created by God; therefore every fact can only be known in reference to God. In the phrase of Van Til, God must always be "the final reference point in all human predication."[4] Every single fact in all space and time can only be known if it is referred to God in its very definition; that is the essence of the Christian principle, the biblical way of reasoning about the universe and all that it contains.

By sharp contrast, the very essence of the non-Christian position—which includes all modern culture in its manifold variety—is to see the universe and the facts which it contains in reference only to humanity. Radical human autonomy is the basis for all modern culture, indeed for

---

3. Van Til, *Christian Theory*, 11.

4. Ibid., 14.

all modern people who inhabit that culture. And the principle which animates their reasoning is to make humanity itself the final point of reference for all understanding of the world, and every single fact which it contains. Again, to use the phrase of Van Til: humanity itself becomes "the final reference point in predication."[5]

There are thus two and only two mutually exclusive views of all reality available to humankind, based on two and only two mutually exclusive principles: the Christian and the non-Christian. One, rightly, refers all facts to the self-contained reality of God; the other, wrongly, refers all facts to the self-defined autonomy of humanity. How then is apologetics possible? How then is fruitful discussion to take place? The thrust of Van Til's primary argument comes right at this point.

The typical apologetics of natural theology has assumed a neutral space between believer and non-believer as a basis for discussion. Van Til seeks to show, however, that there is *no neutral space*. Open discussion between Christian and non-Christian is not possible based upon the illusion of any shared assumptions or possibilities of any kind, be they scientific, philosophical, artistic, or experiential; for in reality all facts in the universe are interpreted either as Christian facts, or as non-Christian facts. The Christian can convince the non-believer only by direct challenge, by confrontation, not by dialogue; the Christian must show the non-Christian that presupposing God as "the final reference point" for all knowledge and experience is absolutely required of all humanity in order to be human. How is this done? By showing the non-Christian that in attempting to deny God, the non-Christian too *must*, despite inner intention, presuppose God's existence, even in order to deny it. God cannot be meaningfully denied unless his existence is first asserted or presupposed; meaningful human experience cannot be upheld on any basis whatsoever, without at the same time embracing the reality of God.

Van Til relentlessly presses home, without compromise, the radical break he intentionally creates between what he calls the Christian position or system, and the non-Christian position or system. If any degree of autonomy is given to humanity whatsoever, it must be stolen from the self-sufficiency of God. And were that to happen, God can no longer be the sole explanatory principle of the universe, the one "reference point in human predication" for all facts in existence. On the other hand, the

---

5. Ibid., 15.

non-Christian is *forced* to put humanity in the place of God, to see humanity as omniscient, and to refer all reality to human omnicompetence. Non-Christian humanity cannot possibly know a fact simply as a fact; all facts must, by compulsion of the very non-Christian principles operative in the assumptions they bring, be brought in relation to unbelieving presuppositions about the universe.

To summarize the basic position: the Christian view presupposes God. And in doing so, it eliminates from the outset the possibility of sharing common ground with the non-Christian view, which operates according to a diametrically opposing presupposition. Yet apologetics—the attempt to persuade the non-Christian— is not to be abandoned; rather, it is to be conducted in a new way. It moves from dialogue to confrontation; the non-Christian must be shown that only the Christian position makes any meaningful human experience whatsoever possible. The non-Christian position is literally "nonsense."[6]

We now proceed to examine more closely several of Van Til's concepts and arguments.

First of all, there is the hard and fast distinction he makes between the Christian way of knowing the world, and the non-Christian way of knowing the world. Again, only these two self-contained options are available; all ways of knowing reality (epistemology) are reduced to this duality (hence our chapter heading). The duality is maintained throughout the book in no uncertain terms. For example, the Bible "is the only standard of truth."[7] By this, Van Til clearly means not simply the truth about God and God's revealed will in Jesus Christ, but every single fact in the universe, embracing all fields of human inquiry. By contrast, the standards of truth used by the non-believer are "false standards"; again, not simply in the affirmation or rejection of the gospel, but in the knowledge of any fact or idea that is knowable, from a philosophical idea, to an aesthetic judgment, to a scientific discovery, to a political decision.

In fact, we need to take Van Til's point a step further. According to his view, the non-believer is *in principle* (the italics are his) "wholly evil."[8] If any truth is discovered by a non-Christian, any truth whatsoever, it is merely "adventitious"; it is due to the "common grace" of God, and not

6. Ibid., 19.

7. Ibid., 43.

8. Ibid., 44.

in any sense whatsoever to the abilities of the non-believer to see rightly any elements of the world around. The Scriptures always say one thing; the non-believer always *in principle* says the exact opposite. The role of apologetics is not in any way to seek to mitigate this opposition; rather, the sheer distinction between the two principles—the Christian and the non-Christian—must be maintained and even highlighted, especially when for the moment they may appear to overlap. The non-Christian cannot—again, in principle, quite literally, *cannot*—see the truth about the world, about God, about humanity, in fact about anything whatsoever.

For example, Van Til offers a brief criticism of Kant, Freud, and Heidegger.[9] While elements of their views may have something like a biblical sound—Kant for example speaks of "radical evil"—Van Til takes great pains to make it clear that apologetics should under no circumstances borrow from or be interested in using such concepts or categories from the non-Christian world. The reason is that they use the non-Christian principle of interpretation of reality to arrive at their conclusion; and that principle of interpretation conflicts with the Christian principle. Only if a view or idea arises from within the Christian principle of interpretation can it have any validity. Indeed, even the same words may be used (like Kant's radical evil), but they in fact have a totally different meaning based on whether they occur in the non-Christian or the Christian principle of interpretation; and again, only these two are available.

It is worth taking a step back for a moment to ask how Van Til sees himself with respect to the tradition of Christian thought, for much of the book is occupied with a rather polemical treatment of major theologians and traditions in church history. To begin with, Van Til finds his initial bearings in the great alternative between the Princeton orthodoxy of B. B. Warfield, and the Dutch "neo-Calvinism" of Abraham Kuyper, an alternative to which he devotes one of the lengthiest chapters in the book. While he expresses great respect for both theologians, in the end a choice must be made: "It is impossible to follow both Kuyper and Warfield, however much lovers of the Reformed Faith may revere them both."[10] Warfield represents the position which Van Til decisively rejects; a position which counts on neutral facts in the universe ascertainable (in a Baconian model) by believer and non-believer alike, and therefore available as a basis

9. Ibid., 54–56.
10. Ibid., 253.

for rationally leading the non-believer to belief. Not Warfield, but Kuyper alone provides the needed backdrop: "It is Kuyper's *Encyclopedie* that has, more than any other work in modern times, brought out the fact of the difference between the approach of the believer and of the unbeliever."[11]

Van Til's reference to Kuyper is, I believer, quite warranted. According to Kuyper in the work mentioned above, there are ultimately two principles, and therefore ultimately two *kinds of people* in the world. The unity of human consciousness itself is rent asunder; one type of humanity has one type of consciousness (the Christian), and the other type of humanity (the non-Christian) has a totally different type of consciousness. How different? "There is an abyss in the universal human consciousness across which no bridge can be laid."[12] Both types are still human, Kuyper concedes; but their inner life is totally different, so that "they face the cosmos from different points of view."[13] And because two kinds of people, therefore two kinds of life; and because two kinds of life, two kinds of philosophy, science, experience, and culture. There is a Christian science, and a non-Christian science; "the two sciences must never be coordinated with each other."[14] We leave Kuyper for now; we will meet him again in a moment when we examine Van Til's view of Scripture more closely.

What is Van Til's attitude to the rest of Christian tradition? The Roman Catholic view ("Romanist") is rejected because it compromises God's self-sufficiency. The Lutheran view is unwilling to accept the final division of all humanity into two classes. As for the Arminianism of evangelicalism, it is "far better than that of Romanism," but nevertheless "infected with something of the same naturalism."[15] Individual theologians fare little better: Justin Martyr he considers the forerunner of Romanist and Arminian views; Irenaeus is unable to work out a fully Christian doctrine, being too much under the influence of Greek philosophy; Tertullian is a Samson who falls in love with the Philistines; the Alexandrians yielded to the temptation of paganism, as everybody apparently knows; Augustine did not really have the answers he thought he had; and of course, modern theology as a whole has eliminated the possibility of ever knowing Christ,

11. Ibid., 301.
12. Kuyper, *Encyclopedia*, 152.
13. Ibid., 154.
14. Ibid., 176.
15. Van Til, *Christian Theory*, 212.

with Karl Barth especially opposed to "historic Reformation doctrine at every point."[16] Of Eastern Orthodoxy there is no mention.

Second of all, Van Til's understanding of Scripture warrants closer examination. On the surface, his view looks quite similar to that of Protestant orthodoxy, both Lutheran and Reformed. Van Til speaks of the Bible as the infallible Word of God; of the necessity of Scripture; of the authority of Scripture; of the sufficiency of Scripture; of the perspicuity (clarity) of Scripture. Each of these concepts can be found in abundance in the early Protestant handbooks of church doctrine. For example, the Reformed classic *Leiden Synopsis (Synopsis Purioris Theologiae*, 1625), likewise mentions the necessity and authority of Scripture in *Disputatio II*, the perfection of Scripture in *Disputatio IV*, and the perspicuity of Scripture in *Disputatio V*. Similarly on the Lutheran side, in his famous *Loci Theologici* (1610), Johann Gerhard speaks in his lengthy treatment of Scripture (*Locus Primus*) of the Bible's authority, perfection, perspicuity, authenticity, and integrity. Are we not then speaking of a similar view of the Bible's authority and function for the life of the church and world?

Yet we must dig deeper. To begin with, it is crucial to understand just *how* Van Til derives and explicates the authority of Scripture. A single sentence shows the shape of his argument: "There would be no *reasonably reliable* [italics his] method of identifying the Word of God in human history unless human history itself is controlled by God."[17] In others words, the doctrine of Scripture itself has a presupposition: which is that God in his power controls all that happens in history. Because God controls all history, all reality conforms to and reveals the plan of God; indeed every fact in the universe occurs because of divine intention, and therefore speaks forth that intention. Now, given such a God, according to Van Til, two things follow. Such a God literally *must* make himself known; and he must do so in an infallible Bible. In other words, the meaning and truth of the Bible are guaranteed by their place within God's control of the facts of the world. The shape of history grounds the authority of Scripture.

Why is this so important? It radically reverses the basic stance of the Reformation understanding of the Bible. As Hans Frei has shown in his brilliant study *The Eclipse of Biblical Narrative*, a complete but subtle reversal of the understanding of Scripture's meaning and truth occurred

---

16. Ibid., 363.

17. Ibid., 28.

in the eighteenth century, under the pressure of the Enlightenment. In the exegesis of early Protestantism, meaning and truth were held together in the world of the Bible; external reality was viewed through the lens of Scripture alone. But then, when access to the facts of the world began to come through other avenues of human discovery, meaning and truth were split apart; the Bible came to mean what it referred to in external reality, as pre-determined by human access to the world. Van Til clearly operates on the near side, the modern side, of that shift; for he makes it clear that the authority of Scripture rests upon its function within the larger world of universal factuality. We do not read the Bible and discover reality; we read God's reality, and discover the meaning and truth of the Bible—so Van Til.

What do we discover? Here again, we must dig even deeper. Van Til speaks repeatedly throughout the book of believing in the "system of truth" taught in the Bible. Again, early Protestant theology too thought very carefully about the system of truth contained in Scripture. Two broad positions emerged (first distinguished by Matthias Flacius Illyricus, in his *Clavis Scripturae*, 1567). The *synthetic* method allowed each doctrinal point (God, creation, humanity, Christ, etc.) to stand on its own as an independent avenue into divine truth; no higher unity was to be sought than the Word of God itself. The *analytic* method started, by contrast, with the goal of salvation as the basic principle of all theology, and all the various articles of faith were rationally aligned toward that goal. Both methods were recognized as orthodox by their practitioners, though subtle theological differences obtained which grew ever greater over time. We are tempted to suppose that when Van Til speaks of the "system of truth" contained in the Bible he is using the older Protestant orthodox formula in one of the two forms.

Clearly, though, he is not. According to Van Til, God made a covenant with Adam in paradise, and through that covenant gave to humanity its task for all time. That task is to regard "the world as a whole as revelatory."[18] In fact, humanity is called to know all facts in the universe, and to arrange them in a system. *Every single fact in the universe* must be known as it relates to God; that is the "system of truth" which the Christian is called upon to know. What about the truths of faith and God's redemptive love, the traditional content of Christian affirmation?

18. Ibid., 15.

We cannot know the truth of the Bible, unless we first know the reliability of the universe; "So *pre-redemptive* [italics his] supernatural revelation is the presupposition of *redemptive* supernatural revelation."[19] In other words, the Christian mandate to know everything—science, art, philosophy, politics, etc., precedes both temporally and logically the Christian understanding of the gospel. Nothing can be left out: "Every fact in the universe is what it is just because of the place that it has in this system."[20]

Once again, the distance of Van Til from traditional Protestant theology needs to be accounted for. How do we get from the goal of Scripture (*finis Scripturae*) being the knowledge and glorification of God and his redeeming love for humanity,[21] to the knowledge of every fact in the universe? We need once again to reintroduce the work of Abraham Kuyper. Against the backdrop of post-Kantian nineteenth-century philosophy, Kuyper developed the notion of a Christian "worldview." The gospel, according to Kuyper, is like the root of a plant; once it grows, it becomes nothing less than a full life-system, encompassing all the ideas and conceptions that make up our entire worldview. Knowledge *has* to include everything, or it is not knowledge. Theologians before Kuyper did not think or speak this way about the gospel, for the simple reason that the *idea* of a worldview is an invention of the nineteenth century.

Van Til takes the idea of a worldview, and makes it the fundamental basis for his apologetics. Christians have one worldview—a view of the universe and everything that it contains; non-Christians have another worldview—another view of the universe and everything it contains; and there can be no compatibility of understanding possible between the two worldviews, for every fact is what it is by virtue of its place within the contrasting systems.

And *third* of all, we need to reflect more closely upon Van Til's conception of the divine-human relationship. God, according to Van Til, is self-sufficient, self-contained, self-explanatory; all three concepts mutually imply one another. Now, there is no doubt that the self-sufficiency of God is indeed a crucial predicate of divine being in early Protestant dogmatics. The influential Reformed theologian Johannes a Marck defines God's independence as "the perfection of God, by which he is

---

19. Ibid., 30.

20. Ibid., 35.

21. So Gerhard, *Loci Theologici*, Locus Primus, 155.

sufficient unto himself, and is the supreme cause of all external reality."[22] Similar statements abound in Reformed and Lutheran, and for that matter Roman Catholic and Eastern Orthodox doctrine. But Van Til mentions *only* God's self-sufficiency, God's self-containment. In traditional dogmatics, self-sufficiency is certainly true of God, but it is far from a complete picture of God, which includes as well his justice, mercy, compassion, etc. The God of the Bible is not only self-contained; the God of the Bible—the divine Trinity—is *self-related*, an eternal communion of love. Severing God's self-containment (his freedom) from God's self-relatedness (his loving) is to lose both.

Does one predicate of God retain its genuine meaning when viewed in isolation from all others? It seems in one respect that even God himself, according to Van Til, is a prisoner of his own self-containment. He argues that the system of truth in Scripture is self-attesting, in such a way that "the testimony or influence of the Spirit in the heart of man cannot be in the nature of new information."[23] In the light of the history of Christian doctrine, this is actually a quite startling statement, for it clearly puts a human limitation on the ongoing activity of God. This idea of a restriction on the role of the Spirit ("cannot") is in sharp contrast to the Reformers, for whom the ongoing work of the Spirit enlivens the inspired word to ever new dimensions of figurative application.

Again, we need to press even a step further. For Van Til, the relationship between God and humanity is a zero sum relationship (if one gains, another loses). Whatever is given to humanity, must be taken away from God; whatever is given to God, must be taken away from humanity. Van Til is clear: "*any* [his italics] measure of autonomy ascribed to man implies a detraction from the self-sufficiency of God."[24] Indeed, it is on this very basis that he dismisses the views of evangelicals, Roman Catholics, and Lutherans. His is a zero sum view of action in the universe; if any real activity is ascribed to humanity, it must be subtracted from God.

Perhaps my observation can be more clearly understood if an alternative view is presented. Two come quickly to mind. In his great treatise *On the Bondage of the Will,* Martin Luther makes it quite clear that humanity has no capacity whatsoever to decide for God, no free will, no

22. Johannes a Marck, *Christianae Theologiae Medualla*, 45.

23. Van Til, *Christian Theory*, 33.

24. Ibid.,14.

liberum arbitrium (for what it is worth, I think Luther is right). The decision of faith is solely a free gift of God's creative Spirit, who works the
miracle of a new humanity. Yet faith, for Luther, is in no sense passive,
inactive, dormant; in his Preface to Romans he writes: "Oh, it is a living,
busy, active, mighty thing, this faith . . . faith is a living, daring confidence
in God's grace, so sure and certain that a man would stake his life on it
a thousand times."[25] And in his commentary on Galatians, Luther can
make the astonishingly bold comment: "Faith is the creator of the Deity,
not in the substance of God, but in us. For without faith God loses His
glory, wisdom, righteousness, truthfulness, mercy, etc., in us; in short,
God has none of His majesty or divinity where faith is absent."[26] No one
can accuse the writer of *On the Bondage of the Will* of the slightest hint
of human autonomy; and yet few speak more eloquently than Luther of
the required response of faith in all its terrible risk and grandeur. All is
of God yes, all indeed; but all from humanity is required as well, literally
all; no zero sum.

The same can be said for Calvin. In the opening chapters of the
Institutes, he sets out the basic theme of the entire work: "Nearly all the
knowledge we possess, that is to say, true and sound wisdom, consists of
two parts: the knowledge of God and of ourselves."[27] He then wrestles with
the question which comes first, and concludes that in fact it is knowledge
of God that grounds all genuine self-knowledge. But the point is: both
are required. It would do us no good at all to understand God, but to fail
to understand ourselves in the light of God; nor to seek to understand
ourselves, but to be ignorant of the living reality of God. The more we
come to know God, the more we grow in self-awareness; the more we
grow in true self-awareness, the more we know God. Again, the two are
not in competition; there is no zero sum.

When Van Til speaks of faith in the system of truth contained in the
Scriptures, he is certainly far removed from the Reformation, for which
faith is complete transformation of existence through encounter with the
risen Christ in the proclaimed word of the gospel.

What then do we mean, in summary, by speaking of the epistemological dualism of Van Til? We mean the division of all humanity into

25. Luther, *Luther's Works*, 35, 370.

26. Ibid., 26, 227.

27. Calvin, *Institutes*, 35.

two camps, believers and non-believers; and corresponding to this, the reduction of all human cultural products to two ultimate and mutually exclusive worldviews, the Christian worldview and the non-Christian worldview. The result of this dualism is that the rhetoric of persuasion in apologetics must yield to a new tone. Van Til speaks the language of challenge; of rejection; of the enemy to be conquered; of enemy territory; of absolute surrender; of a head-on collision, and a struggle for the soul of humankind. The notion of two mutually exclusive worldviews and an ultimate battle between them provides the initial impetus for what will become the movement of Christian Reconstructionism.

CHAPTER 2

Mosaic Law in Society

CORNELIUS VAN TIL HAS created what we might call a conceptual space—as yet empty space—for Christian Reconstructionism. Three elements stand out in the space he has created. First, there are two, and only two, worldviews, the Christian and the non-Christian; all knowledge is divided necessarily into these two systems of truth. Second, God made a covenant with Adam to dominate the earth, and all the basic elements of biblical truth—including even the redeeming work of Christ on the cross—gain their significance only in reference to this creation mandate. And third, the apologetics of conversational dialogue must be swept aside in favor of the rhetoric of confrontation, in which two worldviews meet head-on in a life or death struggle for existence.

The conceptual space is there, though it remains empty in our treatment so far; our next three writers will fill it with content. The ultimate clash of two worldviews—Christian and non-Christian—will take place in three dimensions: social, cultural, and political. We begin with the social, and the book by Rousas John Rushdoony, *The Institutes of Biblical Law*.

The question once again arises: what genre is the book? What kind of book, exactly, is it? The title gives the clue, though the clue is easily missed. A Calvinist can easily be forgiven for assuming some sort of favorable reference to Calvin's well-known masterpiece of church doctrine, *The Institutes of the Christian Religion* (in Latin actually singular, *Institutio*). But that is not the case; the hidden reference rather is to the great legal code of the Roman emperor Justinian, who in the sixth century AD wrote a comprehensive treatment of societal law, the Body of Civil Law (*Corpus iurus civilis*). It is divided into three parts: the Codex, the Digest, and the Institutes; and this third part functions largely as a training manual for students of civil law. Here we find our clue; Rushdoony has written a comprehensive training manual for biblical law.

But we cannot abandon the reference to Justinian too quickly; for the primary thesis of Rushdoony's book is simply this: the *mosaic judicial laws* of the Old Testament are in fact the *civil law* of all societies and nations of the earth. Rushdoony utterly rejects the idea of a "law of nations" (*ius gentium*); in others words, *any* legal system, even any particular *law*, among all nations and peoples of the earth, must come directly from the mosaic laws of the Old Testament. There is *only one law* among all nations and societies; and that is *God's law*, which is given in detail in the various laws of mosaic legislation. Rushdoony calls this divine legislative system outlined in his book a "law-sphere," "law-word," "law-order," or "law-system." The system of mosaic laws constitutes an absolute, abstract, moral law-code, which is comprehensive; and which includes every legislative issue encountered among all peoples of all times and places. This book—in the true spirit of the Roman emperor Justinian— is thus a training manual for the one true civil law of all humankind.

Let us proceed to examine Rushdoony's view in three steps. First, we need to consider more carefully his basic understanding of biblical law, and its function as civil law for humankind. Second, we need briefly to consider his radical rejection of mainline Christianity, and sort out more closely the issues involved in that rejection. And third—and by far the most important element of our focus—we need to summarize his explication of biblical law.

We begin with a simple question: why was the Bible itself written? According to Rushdoony, the Bible was written primarily to aid judges— he means officers of a legal court system—in organizing civil society according to divine law. Any other view of Scripture is "heresy,"[1] a heresy virtually omnipresent in modern Christianity. Those judges who make the decisions which govern the legal proceedings of any society should base all their decisions on the Bible alone; for it is in fact the one true source of all civil law. Everywhere—in all churches and societies—the modern "heresy" has spread that the Bible is not the sole source of civil

---

1. Rushdoony, *Institutes*, 626.

law for society; and the result has been the complete breakdown of law and order. Without mosaic law, society collapses into moral anarchy and falls "into the hands of hoodlums."[2]

Yet even the mosaic law itself has to be set in a broader context. When God created humanity, God gave a mandate to dominate the entire world. The law of Moses was given as a *means* to fulfill that original creation mandate. Thus, the entire law is to be understood through the filter of this one point: God wants humanity to exercise dominion. The coming of Christ does not cancel out that creation mandate, but fulfills it; the call to dominion is therefore still in place. In fact, while it is true that we are justified by grace through faith, we are sanctified, not by grace through faith, but by *law*—the very mosaic legislation which functions as the civil code for all nations. Because it has this particular role within God's creation mandate—the call to dominate the earth—the mosaic law must be understood to include all social reality: legal, civil, capital, labor, property, ecclesial, societal, familial, in fact all forms of human law whatsoever. All law is biblical law, and the only alternative is stark indeed: "the social order which despises God's law places itself on death row: it is marked for judgment."[3] Those who attempt to break this creation mandate will in fact themselves be broken by it. Ultimately, all nations and empires of the world are to be subdued by the church; that is God's mission. In this sacred mission of worldwide dominion, "there is a place for coercion;"[4] and furthermore open warfare is inescapable.

Some of course may wonder whether biblical law and civil law might be a mixture of categories, religious and social. They surely fail to recognize the crucial point, according to Rushdoony, that all law is ultimately religious in nature; that all law taken together, and every single individual law, is fundamentally expressive of an underlying religious principle. Indeed, he can even go so far as to argue that faith itself rests upon a foundation of law, rather than the reverse. Through the divine law, the total life of humankind is ordered under God. God is thus presupposed (remember Van Til's "presupposition") by the legal system. Consequently, the idea of disestablishing religion from any society is impossible. Because the legal system is divinely given, there can be no separation of church

2. Ibid., 3.

3. Ibid., 4.

4. Ibid., 777.

and state; in fact, the idea is not even meaningful, given Rushdoony's overall view. True humanity is exclusively Christian humanity; and true society is exclusively Christian society.

Now, Rushdoony is *not* saying that all societies are in fact Christian; only that all legal systems are inherently religious. However, because of the inherent religious foundation of all law, those not based on the biblical law of Christianity are by definition not only non-Christian, but *anti-Christian*. Thus, there are ultimately two types of legal system in the world: Christian legal systems based on the mosaic legislation of the Old Testament as a divine call to dominate the earth, and anti-Christian legal systems based on the religion of modern humanism. One refers all to God, the other to humankind. There are two primary forms of this modern humanistic heresy: communism and democracy, both equally to be rejected. Modern humanism in both forms is in open rebellion against God; both democracy and communism are under the decadent spell of the ballet, opera house, and art gallery.[5] The goal of Christianity should be to subdue all reality under the divine law order. The world is ultimately a battlefield between the Christian legal system and every anti-Christian legal system (whether democratic or communist); and there are "casualties and wounds" in every such battle.[6]

Old Testament law is to be treated in the form of principles and cases. The Ten Commandments provide the absolute, abstract, legal principles for biblical law. The remaining mosaic legislation functions as a set of "cases" for elaborating those principles. Fuller light can also be shed by the trial of experience. Thus, the primary format of the book is organized around the commandments, one through ten. Under each commandment, first a principle or set of principles is identified; then a series of biblical cases are supplied. Finally, rounding off the presentation is a wide variety of anecdotes from Rushdoony's own personal experience, often drawn from conversations with family members, or from newspaper columns, such as *Dear Abby*.

We need to look secondly at Rushdoony's dramatic, persistent, wholesale rejection of mainstream Christianity, including Roman Catholicism, Protestant Reformation, and Eastern Orthodoxy. Surely anyone who carefully studies *The Institutes of Biblical Law* is struck by how often three

5. Ibid., 7.
6. Ibid., 668.

words recur: heresy, apostasy, and blasphemy. These are of course quite powerful words, and they are directed time and again throughout the book at the major theological traditions of mainstream Christianity, and several of its major theological figures. Both Protestantism and Roman Catholicism are referred to as an "infection" within the church;[7] Luther is "self-tortured, guilt-ridden" even "bloated", and led a Reformation that was "stillborn;"[8] Calvin views are "heretical nonsense," whose reasoning is "silly and trifling;"[9] the Westminster Confession of Faith is guilty of nonsense, breeding "spiritual eunuchs."[10] This is only a sampling of a major strain of lavish criticism throughout the book. Why the animus?

In a single word: the charge Rushdoony makes against mainstream Christianity in all forms is *antinomianism*, which ordinarily means rejection of the divine law. Now, on the face of it, the charge seems highly improbable. After all, Thomas Aquinas offers a massive and refined treatise on divine Law in the *Summa Theologiae*; Martin Luther gives a brilliant exposition of the Ten Commandments in what many regard as the finest summary of his reformation teaching, *The Large Catechism*; and Calvin's explanation of the Ten Commandments in the *Institutes* inspired countless imitations, but few equals, in the confessional and dogmatic literature of unfolding Protestantism. In fact, the very word "antinomian" was *invented* by Martin Luther in his treatise *Against the Antinomians* (1539). Luther of course spoke against "works-righteousness"; but one of his followers, Johann Agricola, took this to mean that *any* attempt to do good works was detrimental to the salvation of the Christian, and therefore held that the church had no need to preach the divine law. Luther responded by stressing the abiding significance of God's law in the church: "Whoever abolishes the law, abolishes the gospel also (*Qui tollit legem, et evangelium tollit*)."[11] Indeed, Calvin placed sanctification before justification in the order of presentation in the *Institutes*, precisely in order to forestall any such misguided criticism of the reformation proclamation of free grace.And the *Russian Catechism* of Philaret is only one instance of many Eastern orthodox statements which includes a full treatment of

7. Ibid., 651.

8. Ibid., 695.

9. Ibid., 653.

10. Ibid., 553.

11. Quoted in Lohse, *Luther's Theology*, 181.

the Decalogue. Of the Orthodox Church in general, Kallistos Ware points out that the admonition to "follow the commandments" is at the heart of genuine spirituality.[12]

So, either Rushdoony's charge of antinomianism against virtually all mainstream ecumenical orthodox Christianity is patently false, or he is using the word *antinomian* in a peculiar, even idiosyncratic way. The latter is the case, and some historical background is needed to understand his definition. A text from Calvin makes the essential point: "We must bear in mind that common division of the whole law of God published by Moses into moral, ceremonial, and judicial laws. And we must consider . . . what there is in them that pertains to us, and what does not."[13] The division of the law of Moses into these three parts—the moral, comprising primarily the Decalogue; the ceremonial, which includes the entire Old Testament sacrificial system; and the judicial, which involves various food regulations and other matters of communal life—actually originates with Thomas Aquinas, from whom it was picked up by both Lutheran and Reformed confessions. *All* agree that the moral law remains valid for all Christians, for all time (except of course the true antinomians, such as Agricola); *all* likewise agree that the ceremonial law, while valid, is fulfilled in Christ the true lamb of God and perfect sacrifice, and therefore no longer operative; the question arises, though, concerning the third, the judicial law.

Luther and Calvin both very carefully consider the question: do the various legislative laws of the Old Testament apply directly to the civil state? Can they be lifted more or less directly off the pages of the mosaic law, and placed into the civil code of Germany, or Switzerland? Luther answers the question in a short treatise entitled *How Christians Should Regard Moses*, published in 1525, a year of great turmoil and tragedy in his work. It was the year of the explosive and bloody peasant uprising in Germany, and Luther was convinced that one cause of the terrifying ordeal was a misguided attempt to apply Old Testament legislation directly: "But our factious spirits go ahead and say of everything they find in Moses, 'Here God is speaking, no one can deny it; therefore we must keep it.' So then the rabble go to it. Whew! . . . Misery and tribulation

---

12. Ware, *Orthodox Church*, 241.

13. Calvin, *Institutes*, 1502

have come out of this sort of thing."[14] Now, Luther affirms quite clearly that the legislative law of Moses is a grand *model* of justice and equity for all nations. But only a model, not a binding legislative codex: "If I were emperor, I would take from Moses a model for my statutes; not that Moses should be binding on me, but that I should be free to follow him in ruling as he ruled."[15] The problem with applying the mosaic legislation directly is that it is so easily contorted and misconstrued into its exact opposite intention: "They are absurd as they rage and fume, chattering to people, 'God's word, God's word!'"[16] By contrast, subtle theological skill is needed in handling rightly the divine word of life: "One must deal cleanly with the Scriptures."[17]

Calvin's similar view can be summarized with a single quotation, taken from his reflection on church and state in the final chapter of the *Institutes*. The subject is civil law: "I shall in but a few words . . . note what laws can piously be used before God, and be rightly administered before men. For there are some who deny that a commonwealth is duly framed which neglects the political system of Moses, and is ruled by the common law of nations. Let other men consider how perilous and seditious this notion is; it will be enough for me to have proved it false and foolish."[18] A generation after Luther, Calvin was well aware of the dangers of self-deception and violence in pretending to construct a theocracy by mosaic legislation. Thus, for Luther and Calvin, the judicial law of Moses *is* a model of equity and justice, but *not* a law code for immediate use by the state. It is the word of *God*; not a word of earthly princes.

Herein lies the issue upon which Rushdoony condemns not only Calvin and Luther, but Aquinas, Bucer, Melanchthon, even the British evangelical F. F. Bruce; all are antinomian, *in his sense*, because they fail to apply the judicial law code of the Old Testament directly to modern civil law. Their views *in toto* are "blasphemous" (oft-repeated throughout the book), and lead directly to "the crime and perversion of the Marquis de Sade," and in the twentieth century to "Lenny Bruce and the hippies."[19]

14. Luther, *Luther's Works* 35, 169.

15. Ibid., 166.

16. Ibid., 174.

17. Ibid., 170

18. Calvin, *Institutes*, 1502.

19. Rushdoony, *Institutes*, 683.

Traditionally, an antinomian is one who denies the continuing validity of the Ten Commandments for Christians; for Rushdoony, an antinomian is one who refuses to apply mosaic judicial legislation directly to the civil code of a society. I think it is fair to say that virtually no major theological figure uses the word *antinomian* the way Rushdoony does; but having understood what Rushdoony means by it, the thrust of his attack on mainstream Christianity becomes clear.

We turn now, thirdly, to a summary of Rushdoony's explication of the mosaic "law-system," which he presents in the form of abstract "moral principles" followed by "case law." We need to keep in mind that he is not merely articulating a descriptive statement of mosaic law; at the same time, he is offering a prescriptive civil law code for every human society. Let me stress: I am not now raising the question whether his vision is faithful to the divine command given in Scripture—as crucial as that question will be. Whether his explication represents the moral vision of God's new world in the Bible, or a religious dystopia of all-too-human origin remains a burning question.

The first commandment (You shall have no other gods before me) articulates the principle that because there is one God, there is only *one law* for all nations and peoples. All who look to any other law except mosaic legislation for their civil code commit blasphemy; they worship an idol. Because there is only one God—one law, the admission of multiple legal systems among nations amounts to polytheism, the worship of many gods; and in fact all modern states, and all modern churches ("Roman Catholic, Greek Orthodox, Lutheran, Calvinist, and all others virtually") are guilty of apostasy.[20] This "heresy" of polytheism has deeply infected the entire church, resulting in the complete moral collapse of Christendom as a whole. Several aspects of case law follow from this basic principle. All education of any kind must be religious in nature, and founded on the Bible: "anything other than a Biblically grounded schooling is thus an act of apostasy."[21] The modern state—whether democratic or communist—is completely to be rejected as totalitarian "statism" (used throughout the book). If God is God, then the state cannot claim any jurisdiction at all over such matters as welfare, religion, family, education, business, agriculture, capital, and labor. The modern state is in fact the antichristian state,

20. Ibid., 18.
21. Ibid., 21.

because of its failure to abide by the divine law. The foundation of the true state is in fact God's law-system, and here idolatry cannot be permitted. While the unbeliever or the heretic does not deserve the death penalty, the idolater—one who leads others astray as a false prophet—must be put to death. Under the modern totalitarianism of democracy, the state administers welfare and education; but in a genuinely godly civil order, it is only those best instructed in the divine law who should carry out these duties. The law upon which all society is built is the tithe, which is not a gift to God but God's own tax to humankind for the use of the earth; the tithe should be collected by the state, but administered only by those who pay it, not by the state. Only in recent times under modern atheistic government has the state stopped gathering the tithe. No property tax is allowed under God's law-system; any such tax brings swift divine judgment upon a nation. Because the tithe is administered by those who give it, and not by the state, the state is in fact very limited indeed; but the modern "antichristian state makes itself god and therefore sees itself as the source of both law and power."[22] More and more, the democracies are at war against orthodox Biblical faith, according to Rushdoony; yet such states are in fact committing national suicide.

The second commandment (You shall not make yourself an image) makes it clear that the truth of a religion is the life of a society. People are not free to worship, or not to worship, without radical consequences for society as a whole. If the religion of a society is false, then that society is by definition headed for total destruction. Either a society will maintain Christian faith as its sole religion, and thereby establish and maintain the godly law and order required; or, a society will embrace humanistic democracy, in which case the people will become active traitors to all genuine law and order. Christian or humanist; life or death: that is the choice. Case law follows. The ancient Temple in Israel was not, as is commonly thought, a house of worship; it was a regal palace, from which God exercised his government over society. Central to this divine governing function was and is the death penalty, which remains in effect in a godly order of society. (Rushdoony lists in this chapter the biblical cases for capital punishment; he lists them again two more times in the book, so I will treat them further below.) Rushdoony is insistent that absolutely *everything* rests on the

22. Ibid., 61.

death penalty: "If capital punishment is not basic to God's law, then Christ died in vain."[23] Protestant and Roman Catholic church leaders who oppose the death penalty are openly defying and despising the law of God, and holding the cross of Christ in utter contempt. In fact, history as a whole is on a disastrous course because society will not cleanse the land of evil by routinely enforcing the death penalty; God himself will therefore cleanse the land of its citizens. Those who break the law lose their citizenship in the state; in fact, condemned criminals have no legal existence whatsoever. No prostitutes or homosexuals are allowed to be citizens of the state; in fact homosexuals are to be regarded as "outside the race of man."[24] The main point is: criminal irresponsibility results in the loss of all rights whatsoever. The reason is that the biblical law-order is in a constant state of war involving two mutually exclusive principles, the Christian and the humanistic; it must carry out that war to its conclusion using all its weapons. Indeed, the war is now a "total war."[25] Egalitarianism—the idea that everyone should have the same opportunities and possibilities in life—is thoroughly unbiblical. In a godly society, the law always discriminates; it always decides who are the legitimate and the illegitimate members of society. The idea of equality is a product of modern democracy, which is the worship of an idol. Democracy has to be called what it is: a heresy: "The heresy of democracy has . . . worked havoc in church and state, and it has worked towards reducing society to anarchy."[26]

The third commandment (You shall not take the name of the Lord in vain) embraces the principle that the law only has a negative function, not a positive function. (It may help to clarify Rushdoony's restriction by pointing out that Calvin, for example, teaches that the negative of the commandment always implies the positive; that "thou shall not kill" implies a positive "reverence for life.") One cannot, for example make the health and welfare of the people the purpose of law; that is a positive function. Law has no function other than to negate; and the implication of this is the limited nature of the law, and therefore the limited nature of the state. The third commandment is hence a broad condemnation of the

23. Ibid., 76.
24. Ibid., 90.
25. Ibid., 95.
26. Ibid., 100.

modern totalitarian state, including modern democracy. If this negativ-ism of the law is ever successfully replaced by a positive function (such as the general welfare of the people), then a complete revolution against Christianity will be the inevitable result. Case law includes the death pen-alty for children who curse their parents, as well as for anyone who takes God's name in vain. Rushdoony admits that such biblical laws are rarely enforced now (!); and laments that women have become increasingly addicted to swearing (!). Swearing in aboriginal societies can be over-looked, because they are already on such a low social level (!). According to Rushdoony, it needs to be stated plainly that contemporary preaching, without qualification, is utterly blasphemous because of its denial of the faith. In fact, the entire world is moving toward a condition of total blas-phemy; and the only future possibility is the divine catharsis of judgment.

According to Rushdoony, the fourth commandment (Remember the Sabbath) is not primarily about a day of *worship*, but about a day of *rest*. Rest means recognizing God's control of all things, and refusing the perverse attempt at human control; whether in the form of Marxism or democracy. Rushdoony is willing to concede that the death penalty no longer applies for those who break the Sabbath law—for those who fail to rest on the Sabbath. Nevertheless, with failure to honor the Sabbath comes slavery, socialism, and "welfarism," all of which are forbidden to the Christian. The Sabbath command to rest includes the modern tech-niques of agriculture, which are thoroughly condemned. The science of agriculture is an unbelieving assault on creation. As opposed to science, the real answer to modern predicaments involving unworthy land-use comes only from the agricultural labor of God's people. That is not to be confused with church people; those who confuse the Sabbath with wor-ship at church "have no knowledge of its meaning."[27] Nations which fail to honor the Sabbath command *are* under the death penalty; they are quite literally doomed to die. All genuine work takes the form of an at-tempt to fulfill the "creation mandate," which is to dominate the earth. Yet only believers can truly make such a contribution to God's Kingdom. "Godly dominion" is the meaning of the Sabbath; on the Sabbath day, those who exercise dominion rest. Rushdoony radically condemns the civil rights movement, labor unions, and native Americans, for being "Non-Christian," and having no concept of work.

27. Ibid., 144.

The fifth commandment (Honor your father and mother) is about
the authority of the family. The Biblical doctrine of the family, according to Rushdoony, has been extensively undermined in modern communism and democracy. The family is central to the biblical way of life.
Above all, it is Darwinian evolution which has attacked the family; and
evolutionary teachers, clergy, and social scientists are responsible for the
breakdown of the family in modern unbelieving society. The ultimate
aim of Darwinianism is to destroy the family as a means to destroying
private property; for in the Bible, the family is the one locus of all private
property. The biblical doctrine of the family is "God-centered"; whereas,
humanism sees family as a social institution to be set aside in favor of
the state. In the Bible, the family has the primary role of carrying out the
creation mandate of dominion over the world. Man has dominion over
woman; and the family has a *possessive* function over the whole earth.
The role of humanity as family is to exercise power over the whole world;
the family is appointed as God's governing authority. The family is thus
the primary unit of *government* in the divine law-system. In all modern
states, this authority as government has wrongly been transferred to the
state. Above all, the family guarantees the right to private property. The
word *property* is now looked down on because of world-wide socialism:
"Thus, most women would bridle at being described as *property*. But the
word *property* should be regarded instead as a . . . very affectionate term
rather than a cold one."[28] The fact is, both wife and children are "property"
of the man. The family alone—not the state—is the only proper organ for
welfare, education, and inheritance. Thus, public education by the state
is utterly forbidden, and anti-biblical; even education by the church is
completely wrong. Only education within the *family* is the way of God.
Above all, state-sponsored public education destroys masculinity and
femininity: "the abandonment of a family-oriented education leads to the
destruction of masculinity, and it renders women . . . aggressive com-
petitors to men."[29] Young girls who refuse their submissive role receive
harsh treatment indeed: at least in the Bible "no . . . girl could become an
incorrigible delinquent and . . . remain alive."[30] Males must be taught their
proper role of dominion, and that can happen only in family-sponsored

28. Ibid., 175.
29. Ibid., 184.
30. Ibid., 187.

education. All welfare should come from the family not the state; state welfare is a violation of God's law, and only leads to deterioration of character. The destruction of the family's ultimate authority in all these realms spells the complete destruction of society itself. The family is not part of a social system; it *is* the social system. Dominion is the primary call of humanity over earth; dominion is the primary operative principle of male "leadership" in the family. Thus, the father, as the source of authority in the family, should normally gain custody of children in a divorce. Women who gain anything by equal rights are openly hostile to Christian law. Modern humanistic democracy is at war against the family, while protection is extended to "perverts and lawbreakers."[31] Modern democracy is a new god, which has replaced the true God of the Bible with the people.

The sixth commandment (Thou shalt not kill) is largely consumed with a much belabored defense of the death penalty. The complete list of "Biblical cases" for the death penalty is listed three times in Rushdoony's book.[32] But other issues are involved in this commandment. For example, the sixth commandment teaches the principle of the *police power of every citizen*, which is essential to Christian law-order. Every citizen must have the right and duty of law enforcement. But focus on the death penalty dominates his treatment. The death penalty not only can, but must be sought in those cases which fall under the biblical mandate. There can be no reverence for life for the believing Christian, only reverence for God. Reverence for life is an "anti-biblical principle."[33] God's law-order requires the death penalty, and there is at present a religious war against it: humanism is at war with Christianity; and the state, the church, and the public school system are all on the side of humanism against Christianity. Whipping from one to forty lashes should be used for minor offenses. There can be no prison system; the prison system is a humanistic device. No prisons should be allowed in society under God's law. There can be no insanity plea for the death penalty, and even children found guilty must be executed. The death penalty should be given to habitual criminals, to homosexuals (homosexuality itself being their crime, according to Rushdoony), to those unable to make bail, to blasphemers, to those who commit incest or bestiality, to those who propagate false doctrines,

31. Ibid., 208.

32. Ibid., 77, 235, 402.

33. Ibid., 222.

to those who sacrifice to false gods, to anyone who refuses to abide by a court decision. Incorrigible delinquents among youth should be given the death penalty. While some who are innocent may inadvertently be put to death, the answer is simply to accept the fallibility of the system: "justice has rough edges, but there is no alternative to justice."[34] Hostility to the death penalty is hostility to God's law. Nations which reject the death penalty are themselves, as a nation, under God's death penalty. The penalty of death arises necessarily out of the very nature of theocracy. Because the death penalty is administered by the state, Rushdoony uses the sixth commandment to describe the role of the state under God's law-order. The state must above all be a Christian state; just as family, church, school, and all things must be Christian. The modern state has failed to require this fidelity to Christianity, and has therefore been surrendered to apostasy and the devil. The state has no role in public welfare, or any major social functions. According to Rushdoony, "some people are slaves and will always be so;"[35] it is only socialism which tries to secure freedom and welfare for all. Anyone who receives welfare from the state must lose their citizenship, including the right to vote. The state has no role whatsoever in welfare, education, or other social functions, which are all reserved only to the godly; its only role therefore is to maintain the military and the courts. The consequence is a very small state, with a very small bureaucracy. The state can require for itself a minimal head tax and no more; "the power to tax in the modern world is the power to destroy."[36] Other case law: homosexuals are not only criminals; it is against God's law even to be friends with a homosexual. There can be no mixing with homosexuals; just as there can be no inter-racial, inter-religious, or inter-cultural marriages. Even organ transplants violate the divine mandate against the principle of "hybridization." There can be no such thing as *social justice* (or injustice); all justice is only individual. Failure to recognize this is leading to the complete dechristianization of society. God not only hates sins, he hates sinners; even more, God requires that *we* hate them (not just their sins) if we are to be faithful to God. Even a "false teaching" at a women's Bible study group is cited with the following prescription: "To defy the law and treat it with contempt, to place oneself above the

34. Ibid., 236.
35. Ibid., 251.
36. Ibid., 284.

laws of God and man, is to be at total war with God and man, and the penalty is death."[37]

The seventh commandment (You shall not commit adultery), is of course designed to protect marriage, but its primary purpose lay elsewhere according to Rushdoony. He is quite explicit: "Thus, a general principle of subjection and service is affirmed, and marriage is then cited as illustrative of this principle."[38] The abstract legal *principle* involved is the necessity of subjection and service rather than autonomy, a necessity which is ontologically constitutive of humanity. Marriage is simply an instance of this principle, a case. Any denial of this biblical "principle of subjection" leads necessary to social chaos. Marriage is not based on romantic feelings, but on hierarchical subjection. In fact, the entire cosmos operates according to this principle of submission to authority. Woman should expect to take second place in a man's life to his work; "he will love her with a personal warmth and tenderness as no other person, but a man's life is his work, not his wife."[39] Women can claim neither priority nor equality. The family is an ultimate law-order, and must enforce discipline on its members. This includes, as we have seen already, the death penalty for juvenile delinquents. If a child does not show proper respect to a parent, that child is simply to be "written off . . . as unworthy of attention."[40] Adultery, as we have already seen, is a capital offense, punishable by mandatory death. The reason for the centrality of the family in "Biblical law" is the need to protect private property, whose "custodian" the family is, and which is the foundation for a healthy society. In fact, the biblical family is really like a corporation. It "pays out dividends to the children in care, support, and inheritance."[41] Because of this corporate function of the family in owning property, the state *cannot* own property, only the family can. What Rushdoony calls "homosexual culture" is everywhere, including vulgar styles, subversive attitudes, the world of art and fashions, in fact the entire outlook of modern intellectuals. We have already seen Rushdoony's fate for homosexuals: "God's penalty is death, and a godly

37. Ibid., 326.
38. Ibid., 333.
39. Ibid., 345
40. Ibid., 362.
41. Ibid., 417.

order will enforce it."[42] Homosexuals who claim to be Christian are not to be believed. *All* notions of equality are to be rejected as evil, including gender equality, and "racial amalgamation." Men in uniform should not be permitted to push a baby carriage.

The eighth commandment (You shall not steal) is actually about the basic human calling and nature to dominate: "*Dominion* is thus a basic urge of man's nature [italics his]."[43] Modern "liberals" have become afraid of this idea of power and domination; but in fact to dominate the earth is the essence of being human. Rushdoony stresses: "This point is of very great importance. Apart from it, the gospel is perverted. Man has a God-given urge to dominion, to power."[44] God's law is given merely as a *means* to dominion; but dominion is the goal, and therefore the proper purpose of the law. This urge to dominion finds its expression primarily in property. Property is given by God to humanity as its rightful godly order of dominating the earth. The church "socialists" who fail to recognize this have simply abandoned the Scriptures. The gold standard should be used in accordance with the Bible. Bankers should not be mistrusted, as they so often are by "socialists"; still, godly people will only take out short-term loans, never long-term loans. Interest-free loans should be given to believers, but not to unbelievers. All employers should be allowed to discriminate on the basis of faith commitment. More case law: daughters should not care for elderly parents unless included in their will, since such patient suffering for an ungrateful parent would not be "godly." In fact, children have no obligation to care for parents who are unbelievers, or who are "militant liberals."[45] There is in God's law-order no such thing as unconditional love. State supported public education is itself a form of theft, for it steals public character. Only those who own property should have the right to vote. All government administrative agencies—such as labor, food and drug, environmental protection—are designed by "modern liberals" to replace Biblical law, and of course must be abolished. The basic principles of modern unionism are inherently anti-Christian. An employer has a "property right" to employ whomever he wants, and may use any grounds to discriminate, including "color, creed, race, or national

42. Ibid., 425.
43. Ibid., 448.
44. Ibid., 450.
45. Ibid., 482.

origin."[46] The Bible is for private capitalism, and against state capitalism; and the acquisition of "godly wealth" is a basic fulfillment of the divine purpose. The biblical law of hospitality to strangers no longer applies in modern society; for it would require the re-ordering of a person's private life under modern conditions.

The ninth commandment (You shall not bear false witness) does not mean having to tell the truth. For example, Christianity must oppose the use of the polygraph by anyone, whether voluntary or not, as a breach of God's law system. Truth-telling is only necessary in fact in certain contexts. Rushdoony uses the ninth commandment as an occasion to condemn the *Westminster Confession* for not telling the "truth" about sanctification, since it ascribes it to grace, rather than law. In fact the whole Reformation lied in this regard (the *Formula of Concord* receives similar treatment). All who teach a defective view of Scripture are deemed traitors. All courts are religious establishments; and one result of this is that the religious beliefs of all witnesses can be questioned under oath. The First Amendment of the United States Constitution does not in fact guarantee freedom of religion; it only means that the *federal government* cannot legislate in matters of religion, which right is reserved to the states. The true goal of this amendment must be for states to set up God's "law-order." Churches which do not strive to set up God's law-order in society are simply liars. The office of judge in a law-court is a theocratic office; the minister is to declare God's Word, and the judge is to apply it legally. Ungodly judges, having no such standard, must be excluded from the bench. Every judge should undergo theological training, and not the "humanistic" education offered in modern law schools. Denial of this is of course heresy.

The tenth commandment (You shall not covet) forbids all forms of fraud and deceit. We now live in an unhappy time in which "the character of people is delinquent and degenerate."[47] Any form of welfare is the basis for an "anti-God society," since the law takes from one and gives to another without God's sanction. That does not mean that there can be no special privilege in society, a much-abused concept according to Rushdoony. No society can ever hope for total equality, nor should it attempt it. God does not will it. In a biblical form of society, family, free enterprise, and indi-

46. Ibid., 510.
47. Rushdoony, *Institutes*, 639.

vidual initiative are given special privilege. Thus, families, organizations, and employers can exercise any sort of discrimination they wish to foster special privilege, as they see fit; and the state must not, cannot, interfere.

In conclusion, we ask: is Rushdoony's portrayal *truly* "the law of the Lord" which is "perfect," " "reviving the soul," "making wise the simple," "rejoicing the heart," "enlightening the eyes" (Ps. 19: 7–8)? Or is it rather an unspeakable nightmare of death, repression, violence, hatred, bigotry, discrimination, and yet more death? At some point, the question must be honestly faced.

CHAPTER 3

Cultural Christianity

To RETURN TO VAN Til once again; a conceptual space was created giving shape to an absolute clash between two—and only two possible—complete systems of thought and action, or "truth-systems." The absolute contrast between the two systems is essential to Van Til, and to Christian Reconstructionism as a movement; and so also are the metaphors of warfare, violence, struggle, clash. Cohabitation is not an opposition; compromise is evil; consensus is forbidden; one must win, the other must lose, in its totality. Rushdoony first fills the conceptual space with content by arguing that the judicial laws of the Old Testament are in fact a civil codex for every human society, and that the Christian church, if it is to remain Christian, must enforce that codex in its entirety upon everyone. Rushdoony scathingly rejects the mainstream orthodox Christian position of Thomas Aquinas, Martin Luther, John Calvin, and countless others, in which the judicial laws are received as a model of divine justice, but not as a full blueprint for a total society. It is either/or; either, the church and society (everywhere) follow the legal system Rushdoony sets out, or, both church and society lapse into open blasphemy.

Until now in our study, the conceptual space created by Van Til is filled solely with a legal system, albeit a comprehensive society-embracing "law-structure." The conceptual space created by Van Til will now be filled out even further by our third book, *A Christian Manifesto*, by Francis Schaeffer. As we will see, Schaeffer argues that Christianity is not limited simply to a legal system, but in fact embraces an entire culture. Christianity belongs to that culture; and that culture belongs to Christianity. This unity—if not identity—between Christianity and a particular human culture gives us the title of our chapter, and certainly impels the momentum of Christian Renconstructionism forward with driving force. Van Til's model of two ultimate clashing systems of truth is retained and expanded; and the metaphors of violent conflict spill over into literal truths.

Now, it is true that Schaeffer never directly identified himself as a Christian Reconstructionist. The reasons for including him in this volume however are amply warranted. He studied under Van Til, and helped to popularize the notion of "Christian presuppositionalism" for a wider audience. Furthermore, he applied the notion of a Christian "worldview" encompassing all reality—first advanced by Kuyper—to the various fields of art, literature, philosophy, sociology, science, ecology, and so forth: again, in a popular vein, with broad appeal. He warmly appreciated the contribution of Rushdoony, and the difference between them is largely attributable to narrow and peripheral issues of conservative evangelical eschatology stemming from the nineteenth century, not to the central themes of Christian involvement in society. I suppose if Schaeffer had never written *A Christian Manifesto* his inclusion within this study would be unnecessary. The fact remains, however, that he did write it; and in doing so, took a decisive and massively influential turn toward the politicization of the gospel that speaks loudly and clearly in behalf of a Christian reconstruction of society.

Why the title of the book? On the page before the title page, two other manifestoes are referred to, and that of course gives us our clue not only to the meaning of the title, but to the nature of the book as well. The first referred to is *The Communist Manifesto* of 1848, the attempt by Marx and Engels to convert the economic, social, and political ideas of Marx into a movement of the people, into *communism*. The second referred to is the (surely less well known) Humanist Manifesto (I and II, 1933 and 1973—a third actually appeared in 2003, after Schaeffer's death), in which the "religion of humanity" is heralded as the solution of all social problems, a new *humanism*. By setting his own "manifesto" in this series, Schaeffer is offering Christianity as the third -ism, competing in the marketplace of ideas alongside communism and humanism. Moreover, as in the case of the other two, he has attempted to convert the *ideas* of Christianity into a *social movement*; for in his view, only such a call to action can save Christianity from the precipice of failure upon which it currently balances so precariously.

According to Schaeffer the primary failure of Christianity—he blames both mainstream and evangelical thinkers—is the inability or unwillingness to see Christian "Truth" (always capitalized by Schaeffer in this context) in its all-encompassing totality. Christianity cannot view the world in fragments; it must necessarily see the world comprehensively. Schaeffer uses the word "worldview" to communicate his conception of Christianity; there is a Christian worldview, and it includes literally everything, all that exists, all reality. The idea of a Christian worldview, as we have seen, ultimately goes back to Abraham Kuyper; but there is a subtle difference in the derivation of the Christian worldview between Schaeffer and Kuyper which needs at least to be recognized.

For Kuyper, the idea of a Christian worldview is ultimately based on the nature of human consciousness. Because human consciousness is like a plant that grows from inner seeds to full fruition, the gospel cannot remain limited, but must necessarily expand to the full life system it represents. Kuyper's thought is hence fully imbedded in the theology of consciousness popular in the nineteenth century, ultimately derived from Schleiermacher. Schaeffer arrives at the same result—a Christian view of everything—but by a different approach. Because Jesus Christ rules all things, therefore Christianity is the Truth about all things. Notice: there is no gap, for Schaeffer, between Christ the Lord on the one hand, and those who serve him on the other. For Schaeffer, saying Christ rules everything necessarily means that Christians know everything; they cannot just know "individual truths" but must know the "Truth about all of reality."[1] There is no distance between the Lord of all reality (which all mainstream orthodox Christians confess) and the notion that Christians know the truth about everything (not embraced by orthodox Christianity). Christians have from the very beginning professed: Jesus Christ alone is the Truth (cf. John 14:16). They have not made the corresponding claim of Schaeffer: Christians know Truth about all reality.

Let me illustrate. In his discussion of the doctrine of creation, the Reformed orthodox theologian Johannes Wollebius makes the following typical distinction: "We shall leave to students of the physical world (*physicis*) the problem of describing the various creatures. For us, it is

---

1. Schaeffer, *Manifesto*, 20.

sufficient to list them according to the days of creation."[2] His point is: Christian theology has a vital interest in confessing the glory of God's creative power, which brought forth the world out of nothing, and sustains it by his wisdom; it does not however have any special interest in or knowledge of the morphology of plants and animals, which belongs to the province of natural science. Now, this is just the kind of thinking—widely held in classical Christianity—that Schaeffer not only rejects but castigates; such thinking in "bits and pieces" has almost brought Christianity to ruin. No, Christianity alone knows the truth about science, philosophy, law, government, film, music, literature, in fact all reality, because it is a worldview. Again, *every* mainstream Christian would agree that *Christ rules* all these things, and much more; in fact the entire universe. But no one before Kuyper would have even ventured to suggest that Christians alone *know all these things* for the simple reason that the idea of a worldview did not exist until Kant; and the idea of *Christian* worldview until Kuyper. Schaeffer takes this one idea, and pushes it to the extreme limit possible.

How far does he push it? According to Schaeffer, some Christians are willing to confess their belief in the truth of the gospel. They believe, for example, in the truth of creation, the virgin birth, the miracles of Christ contained in the Bible, the redemptive work of Christ on the cross, the final hope of his consummation. But for Schaeffer this is not enough. They are believing in the truths of the gospel; they are not believing in the concept of Truth itself, which is equivalent to all reality. Logically stated, for traditional doctrine it is the content of Christian faith—the gospel—which defines what Christians mean by "truth"; for Schaeffer, it is the concept of truth—Truth—which defines the content of the gospel. The concept of truth does not come from within the witness of Christian faith; rather, it grounds that witness in a logically prior understanding of truth as an all-embracing worldview, an understanding which ultimately derives from the post-Kantian world of the late nineteenth century. Interestingly, the logical move made by Schaeffer—locating Christian doctrine in a wider concept of meaning and truth—is made in the exact same way by nineteenth-century Protestant liberalism, although of course with different theological results.

---

2. Wollebius, *Compendium*, 54.

The great opponent of the Christian worldview for Schaeffer is of course secular humanism. Humanism too is a worldview (according to Schaeffer), an all-embracing system of reality; and over the course of the twentieth century it has come to dominate society in the United States and Europe. There has emerged a humanist elite that has effectively silenced all criticism, and become the judicial and governmental authoritarian force promoting anti-Christian state action. There once was a Christian worldview dominant in both Europe and America (more on this shortly); but over the course of a century the humanist worldview has all but eclipsed the last vestiges of this Christian consensus in the West. The two worldviews—Christian and humanist—are not only opposite in every way, producing opposite results in every feature of society; according to Schaeffer they *inevitably* produce opposite results. It is not even metaphysically possible for Christianity and humanism to coexist; one must live, the other must die, and the death struggle is now in its final stages. They are not simply two separate worldviews, but two separate *entities*; and any sort of mixture not only has not happened, but cannot possibly happen under any circumstances. They have "total differences in regard to society, government, and law."[3]

What kind of a world does the entity of "humanism" promote as Schaeffer sees it? Its ultimate aim is a form of "slavery" under the state. Humanism now controls the consensus in society, and also the media. What is taught in public schools is a form of indoctrination by humanism; and the various departments of government are completely suffused by a humanist agenda. Under humanism, all laws are simply arbitrary, because they are not measured against the written law of Moses. The efforts of humanism amount to a "takeover of government and law" from Christianity in the West.[4] Modern science once used to be a Christian enterprise, but now it too has become humanistic. Authoritarian domination is the ultimate goal of humanism, which has already reached extremely far along that road. Even public television regularly "indoctrinates" its unsuspecting viewers with the anti-Christian, humanist worldview. Humanism has brought "punk rock . . . nihilism, hopelessness, meaninglessness of life, anarchy."[5] Soon enough, an elite will take over, probably resembling the

---

3. Schaeffer, *Manifesto*, 21.
4. Ibid., 39.
5. Ibid., 76.

Roman Empire under Caesar Augustus. The totalitarian state is already here, and is clearly already being enforced in the public school system in the United States. Its only claim to authority is naked power; for humanists only obey the state because the state has weapons.

How has it come to this? And what is the alternative? According to Schaeffer, the West—meaning Europe and the United States—is founded on a Christian cultural consensus, or Christian worldview. Western culture is Christian; and Christianity is imbedded in western culture. History shows, according to Schaeffer, that nowhere else does the unique link between Christianity and culture take place but in the West; and efforts to transplant that Christian culture—such as those by the "State Department after WWII"—failed precisely because of the lack of the necessary base. The Christian worldview was once all-pervasive in Europe and America, but now humanism has taken its place. The Christian cultural consensus in the West has fostered a civilization greater than any other in human history, though it is on the verge of disappearing. Only the "Judeo-Christian" culture has produced genuine human freedom. Schaeffer (with Rushdoony) believes that the First Ammendment was never intended to separate church and state; rather, its purpose was to keep the federal government from establishing a national church, so that individual states could establish *state* churches without federal interference. Part of this Christian culture in fact is a severely limited state; there is no place in the Christian worldview for what Schaeffer considers the immense power of the modern state. Where humanism always leads to "statism," the Christian cultural consensus always leads to "severely limiting the scope of Federal State authority."[6] And of course, one must choose, one or the other, without mixture or compromise.

To summarize thus far: Christianity and Western culture are two sides of the same coin. Christianity is the foundation of western culture; Western culture is the guarantee of Christianity. The church at large has failed to see this crucial link between faith and the worldview it necessarily generates; and because of this failure open warfare has broken out between the two great rivals for world dominance, Christianity and humanism.

What kind of warfare? With Van Til, whose concerns are largely epistemological, the massive confrontation is between two mutually exclusive

6. Ibid., 115.

worldviews; yet a confrontation that remains largely in the realm of ideas, and how we argue them. With Rushdoony, the focus gains greater definition; the confrontation is between two mutually exclusive legal systems, the mosaic and the humanist, and is largely carried out in the sphere of judicial argument and application. With Schaeffer, the nature and extent of the confrontation takes a new and sharply critical turn. Because Christian culture is now opposed to humanist culture; and there can be absolutely no mixing, absolutely no compromise, absolutely no cross-communication of creative interplay; there is nothing short of a *cultural war*. Christian culture is at war with humanist culture. Even more, there are no neutral parties; either one takes the Christian side, or one takes the humanist side. The choice is stark, and it must be made by everyone, whether they want to or not. Let us examine Schaeffer's "culture war" more closely.

It is a total war; or better, a war of totals. By identifying the Lordship of Christ with the interests of the church; by encompassing the message of the church within the rubric of "culture"; Schaeffer has eliminated by definition any possibility other than total war at the outset. The culture war between Christianity and humanism is not simply a fact, regrettable or laudable as one pleases; it is rather an inevitable, ontologically necessary occurrence. Christianity and humanism must fight; they cannot not fight; because they represent not simply two opposing points of view, but two opposing "entities," two all-inclusive metaphysical forces in the universe: "There is no way to mix these two total world views. They are separate entities that cannot be synthesized."[7] By "cannot" here Schaeffer clearly means more than a factual statement of observation; he means rather a metaphysical truth about two mutually opposing powers in the universe, Christian and humanism, "God and Caesar." Nor is this simply a matter of "religious" controversy, for in speaking of a Christian culture, everything is included in the battle: "We have to understand that it is one total entity opposed to the other total entity. It concerns truth in regard to final and total reality—not just religious reality, but total reality."[8] Thus, the epistemological dualism introduced by Van Til—two and only two mutually exclusive worldviews, Christian and humanist—has become in

7. Ibid., 21.
8. Ibid., 51.

Schaeffer a full-blown metaphysical dualism between two opposing to-talities in the universe.

What is equally clear and important for Schaeffer, Christian culture is desperately losing the war to humanist culture. His timeline varies somewhat throughout the book—did it happen at the beginning of the twentieth century, the forties, the fifties, the sixties, the seventies?—but the point is clear: a radical shift has taken place in which the Christian culture of the West is being totally replaced by secular humanism. We are not quite there yet; but we are almost there, almost to the point where the Christian consensus is lost forever, and humanism takes over once and for all. Schaeffer stresses: this cannot be seen, must not be seen, as a narrow war about religious issues (say, in the manner of older contro-versy about the doctrine of the sacrament or justification by faith alone). Because Christianity is a culture, the war must be a cultural one: the battle must take place across the entire front. Not just religion, but "final reality" is the issue at stake. The battle for Christian culture against humanist cul-ture must be fought in philosophy, art, film; it must be fought against the "secular media," who do not know how to report objectively; it must be fought against all courts, including the Supreme court; it must but fought against public education; it must be fought against the authoritarian elite who are taking over the functions of society; it must be fought against mainstream and evangelical Christians who just don't understand; it must be fought against non-Christian lawyers; it must be fought against the humanist takeover of government functions; it must be fought against the forces of humanism which have "indoctrinated millions" and "infiltrated every level of society."[9] What is at stake is not so much the truth of the gospel, as "the Truth of what is."[10]

Why has it gotten to be this bad? According to Schaeffer, Western democracy is built on a Judeo-Christian cultural base. The two necessar-ily go together: Christianity and democracy, democracy and Christianity. How then has it come to be that humanism, over the course of a century (the twentieth), has well-nigh swept-aside the Christian culture which forms the very basis of democracy in the United States? His answer is simple and straightforward: immigration. The great waves of immigrants who came to the shores of the United States in the mid-nineteenth century

9. Ibid., 53.
10. Ibid., 20.

unfortunately did not bring with them the required Christian cultural basis, especially in its Reformation form. The result was predictable, according to Schaeffer: as more and more immigrants flooded in, the cultural consensus was bit by bit eroded, until now it has finally given way, or is about to. Such immigrants enjoy the freedoms of Christian democracy, but do not have the necessary Christian consensus to fit "rightly" and appropriately within it. Quite simply: immigrants can be blamed for the losing battle of Christian culture against humanist culture.[11]

Needless to say, Schaeffer nowhere remarks upon the all too obvious point that the original Puritan forebearers of his "Christian consensus" were themselves immigrants, and glad to find in the new world a much welcomed home; that indeed they framed their "errand into the wilderness" after the one true movement of glorious immigration in the Bible, which is of course the movement of the people of Israel, led by God through his servant Moses, into the promised land. Without this biblical and historical framework, "immigration" is perceived by Schaeffer as an invasion of non-Christian, or insufficiently Christian, people who undermined the historic Christian culture of the nation, thus unleashing the culture war against humanism.

Given that there is now a cultural war between Christianity and humanism according to Schaeffer; and that this war is an all or nothing struggle between two total entities which not only share nothing in common, but cannot possibly share anything in common; and furthermore given that Christianity is within a hair's breadth of losing the battle against humanism, which encompasses every realm of government, science, law, education, art, film, philosophy, etc.; what are Christians to do about it? This question—addressed in the latter chapters of the book—appears to be the real thrust of Schaeffer's manifesto, which by definition is a call to action. What kind of action is the Christian being called to? There is not one answer to this question but two; and the two unfold in stages. First one approach must be tried, and if that approach fails, the final solution must be applied. The only goal of either approach must be to win the battle, which means the absolute, ultimate defeat of humanism in all its cultural manifestations. Any other outcome would be the worst kind of Pyrrhic victory, shooting over the shoulder in retreat with no real results to show for the effort. No compromise; no consensus; only total victory or

11. Ibid., 134.

total defeat. It will not be easy: "We must understand that there is going to be a battle every step of the way."[12]

The first approach for Christians to try is civil disobedience. It is necessary, according to Schaeffer, because we (he means the United States, upon which he focuses increasingly in the final chapters of the book) have so radically departed from the viewpoint of the "Founding Fathers." The original founding of the country was based on the affirmation of the existence of God; that affirmation is now violently opposed, according to Schaeffer, by the whole humanist system that now rules American society. The government system we have now is *totally different* in every way from that formed by the original framers of our social contract. Currently, people obey the state only because it has the guns; then, people obeyed the state because, as Christians, they were "God-fearing," and knew the state was founded on the Bible. All life—including civil government—comes under the Law of God. The original founders understood this; contemporary government does not. So what is to be done?

According to Schaeffer, when government propounds a law that contradicts the Bible, that government abrogates its authority and is not to be obeyed. When a non-biblical law is upheld by the state, then legitimate authority has ceased; and at that point the Christian not only has the option, but the duty, to disobey the state. The issue is not academic; Schaeffer makes clear: "That is what we are facing today. The whole structure of our society is being attacked and destroyed. It is being given an entirely opposite base which gives exactly opposite results."[13] That is, the Christian base is being utterly destroyed and replaced by a humanist base; and the results are more dire than Christians have faced in the past, even Luther standing up against the corruption of the medieval church.

Civil disobedience at this time in history should primarily take the form of protest, according to Schaeffer. For example, Christians should withhold tax money which might support government actions they consider non-Christian, and be willing to go to jail to pay the consequences. Similarly, "Christian schools" should do everything possible to resist any state entanglement and interference in their affairs; and this might very well involve resisting the Internal Revenue Service. Schaeffer rather blandly points out: "Again there would be trials and possibly jail

12. Ibid., 75.
13. Ibid., 101–2.

for someone."[14] But for protest to be effective, it has to take on extreme measures. Of course, as we have seen, public school education is no longer an option for the Christian, for humanism has made its "worldview" the exclusive standpoint of all public education. The cultural war has to be joined and there is no neutral position: "It is a time for Christians . . . who do not accept the narrow and bigoted humanist views rightfully to use the appropriate forms of protest."[15] After all, says Schaeffer, one must remember the Boston Tea Party. Similarly, protest must take the form of Christian protest against the power of the federal government in favor of state's rights. Christianity means a small federal government; humanism means a large federal government; so Christians must do all in their power to combat federal authority, for the original government of the United States was Christian.

Now, let us take a step back before we proceed to step two. Schaeffer makes it clear that even civil disobedience should only be undertaken after every effort has been made to correct and rebuild society, as he sees it, along the lines of the Christian consensus upon which it once was based. Christian "reconstruction" is truly the first option; only when it is no longer possible, must "we advocate tearing it down or disrupting it."[16] However, having said this, Schaeffer is equally clear throughout the book—indeed the title says it all—that now is the time for Christians to take the next step; to move forward in active combat against the humanist system in its totality. If civil disobedience does not work, a second option—a second and final step—is available.

That option is force; that is, force used against the government, and Schaeffer clearly means the government of the United States of America. If civil disobedience by Christians does not work in restoring God's law— the Christian culture which forms the fabric of American society—then force against the government is not only an option, but a necessary one: "There does come a time when force, even physical force, is appropriate . . . when all avenues to flight and protest have closed . . . force is appropriate."[17] Schaeffer argues that, just as a true Christian in Hitler's Germany should have defied the state with force, so the modern American

14. Ibid., 109. I am not aware that Schaeffer himself ever went to jail for civil disobedience.

15. Ibid., 110.

16. Ibid., 106.

17. Ibid., 117.

Christian is now in a position to use force against the government of the United States, which similarly has become totalitarian ("statist"). For both Nazi Germany and the United States government have abrogated their rightful authority under God's law, and therefore must not only be resisted, but actively and forcefully defied. Since American society has been totally "destroyed" by the false god of humanism, there is nothing left to do but to reply with force, where civil disobedience fails.

Under what conditions should Christians use force against their own government? Needless to say, this is an ominous question, and one would expect an exceedingly cautious and careful answer. Astoundingly, it is not there in Schaeffer's book. Rather, he repeatedly refers—always in italics— to *the bottom line*, by which he means the point at which Christians can and must shift from a tactic of peaceful demonstration to forceful action.

Some historical background might be helpful. Broadly speaking, Christian tradition has held three positions in regard to the use of violence: pacifism, just-war theory, and holy war. Pacifism argues that force is valid under no circumstances whatsoever, and as an absolute position has been a minority option within Christianity. The mainstream has been occupied with a theory of just-war, in which extremely cautious and elaborate rules are established to make it clear exactly under which cases the use of force is justified. By contrast, the minority on the other extreme is the "holy war" notion, in which the use of force in the cause of Christian culture is taken for granted when that culture is under perceived threat.

Schaeffer clearly belongs in the third category; calling for a war of Christian culture against humanist culture, with force against one's own government as an increasingly necessary option. He is aware of the extreme measures he is recommending: "force of any kind is a place where many Christians stop short."[18] Nevertheless, he justifies it in light of the human plight: "In a fallen world, force in some form will always be necessary."[19] He stresses the point that force cannot be left only to the state (a principle of just-war theory); "Such an assumption is born of naiveté. It leaves us without sufficient remedy when and if the state takes on totalitarian dimensions."[20] Again, by totalitarian state he is referring to the United States, as the context of the final chapters of his book makes abun-

18. Ibid., 106.
19. Ibid., 107.
20. Ibid., 107.

dantly clear. In summary: "*the bottom line* is that at a certain point there is not only the right, but the duty, to disobey the state"—and that because the United States is losing, or perhaps has lost, the "Christian consensus" upon which it was founded.[21] Again appealing to the Christian consensus, if basic rights are being attacked by the state, Christians have "a *duty* to try to change that government, and if they cannot do so, to abolish it."[22] The humanist government of the United States is the *only* state under consideration in this section of the book, and the clear aim of such abolition.

Francis Schaeffer in his culminating book unambiguously calls for steps taken against the government of the United States; steps that would abolish the "total world view" of humanism which has in fact captured government, law, media, public education, and society in general; and the use of force as required. The government of the United States has become an "authoritarian" government; and therefore like Nazi Germany, or Stalin's Russia, requires total resistance. Now, surely the question has to be squarely addressed: what exactly does Schaeffer mean by *the bottom line*? And furthermore, under what conditions should force be used? And by whom? And what kind of force? And under what biblical mandate? One is frankly astonished to hear Schaeffer's answer: "What does all this mean in practice to us today? I must say, I really am not sure all that it means to us in practice at this moment."[23] One struggles to understand Schaeffer's silence at precisely the point where the most eloquent deliberation is called for.

To repeat: just-war theory offers a highly reasoned, highly nuanced set of multiple criteria to determine when and if force can be used in the last resort against a massive and overwhelming evil, such as Hitler's fascism. To call for the use of force without meeting those criteria—from a theological point of view—is to engage in unjust violence. Schaeffer nowhere mentions the long tradition (going back to Augustine) of just-war theological reflection in church doctrine, nor the biblical texts on which it is based. His point rather seems to be that the ultimate dualistic conflict between the two total entities—Christianity and humanism—self-evidently justifies the application of force, as if any other option is not even a real possibility: "We have been utterly foolish in

21. Ibid., 120–21.
22. Ibid., 128.
23. Ibid., 131.

our concentration on bits and pieces, and in our complete failure to face the total world view that is rooted in a false view of reality. And we have not understood that this view of reality inevitably brings forth totally different and wrong and inhuman results in all of life."[24] Humanism is so powerful, so evil, and so pervasive in society; that the use of force against it by Christians—"even physical force"—is apparently simply obvious. The culture war is a holy war.

Even Schaeffer realizes that his "call to action," in taking the form of the use of force, might seem to many to cross a line. With almost stunning insouciance, Schaeffer acknowledges that there are plenty of "kooky people around."[25] Yet that does not keep him from holding up as a model, for contemporary Christian resistance to government tyranny in the United States, colonial resistance to British tyranny: "The thirteen colonies reached the bottom line . . . that . . . led to open war in which men and women died."[26] There has to be a bottom line; and it has to be not just a principle, but a call to action, even violent action; and according to Schaeffer, we have reached it.

24. Ibid., 131.
25. Ibid., 126.
26. Ibid., 130.

CHAPTER 4

Christian Political Domination

THE EMERGENCE AND LINKAGE of the four central ideas which constitute Christian Reconstructionism has been cumulative. Each of the works we have studied so far has promoted a theme which has been incorporated into an evolving nexus of thought: epistemological dualism, the direct application of mosaic judicial law to all societies, and cultural Christianity. Our fourth book, *Christian Reconstruction: What It Is, What It Isn't,* by Gary North and Gary Demar, attempts to draw together the major ideas of their predecessors (Van Til, to whom the book is dedicated; Rushdoony, and Schaeffer); and to make as their own contribution the last of the four ideas which make up Christian Reconstructionism as a whole: the idea of Christian political domination, which means a single worldwide Christian "civilization" which encompasses all realms of life and all peoples. While we will try to avoid undue repetition, we will follow them as they draw together the ideas of their predecessors as parts into a whole; and then examine closely and carefully the full meaning of their proposal for a dominant global Christian "civilization."

According to the authors, the primary work of Van Til can be compared to a demolitions expert. By creating an absolute epistemological dualism between Christians and humanists, between the Christian worldview and the humanist worldview (and again there are no other options available), Van Til effectively destroyed the entire edifice of modern culture and society. The absolute irreconcilability of Christianity and humanism; the uncompromising rejection by Christians of all signs of a humanist worldview, wherever they may be found; this destructive force alone made Christian Reconstruction possible. The only problem with Van Til (according to North and DeMar) was the limitation of the negative; he could only destroy everything, and had no time to think about what to build in its place.

Enter Rushdoony. Rushdoony saw the need for reconstructing society on the rubble of humanism by applying directly the legal code of mosaic law. According to the authors, while the idea itself was not new—it had been tried for a while by the Puritans, though ultimately abandoned by them in favor of "Newtonian rationalism"—Rushdoony took this idea to its absolute logical conclusion. There can be no area of "neutrality" in the world; everything that exists is either Christian or non-Christian, divine or satanic. The work of Francis Schaeffer served to destroy the last illusions of "neutrality" in philosophy, education, politics, science, even the writing of history. Every act of culture is either a Christian act or a non-Christian act; every artifact of culture is either a Christian artifact or a non-Christian artifact. No other Christian "movement" really sees this, according to the authors: "Christian Reconstructionism is the only Bible-affirming movement on earth that offers an uncompromising biblical alternative."[1]

As a result of their uncompromising stand for "biblical truth," the various adherents of Christian Reconstruction are being subjected to an "ecclesiastical war," according to the authors. The church is utterly opposed to their views, and will do anything to get rid of them. The church cannot stand to hear the message that biblical law really does apply to everything: to economics, to family life, to civil government, to political systems, to welfare, to foreign policy, and to family relations; all of these are covered by the various legal "sanctions" imposed by the mosaic law of the Old Testament. On the other hand, the authors are convinced that those who oppose them theologically are "incapable" of giving a proper biblical answer. To the whole Christian world they proclaim: "what we have is better than anything they have."[2]

In the meantime, God himself has entered the controversy between Christian Reconstructionism and mainstream confessional Christianity. According to the authors, AIDS is God's own "eloquent response" to the myth of moral and cultural neutrality. There is no neutral ground

1. North and DeMar, *Christian Reconstructionism*, xii.
2. Ibid., xvi.

whatsoever between Christian and non-Christian worldviews; this un-assailable fact has now been demonstrated by God himself through in-flicting AIDS on the world. The various attempts of religious bodies to "silence" the voices of Christian Reconstructionism have often applied various "ecclesiastical maneuvers"; but AIDS as a divine response is a problem that "Robert's Rules of Order won't solve."[3] All critics of Christian Reconstructionism—that is to say, those Christians in the mainstream of historic Christianity—are deemed "antinomian."

Two forces are thus currently at work in the contemporary world, according to North and DeMar. On the one hand, Christian Reconstructionists are hard at work applying the law of God as a tool of world dominion. The mosaic law covers every sphere of life: personal, spir-itual, intellectual, and cultural. The goal of Christian Reconstructionism is to advance that dominion progressively through every sphere, through every nation, among all peoples of the earth. *How* that will happen is the primary theme of the book. It can only happen, though, when Christians at large finally and once-for-all admit that there is absolutely *no common ground* between believers and non-believers; failure to "admit" this is the reason why mainstream confessional Christianity as a whole is "antinomi-an." The various paradigms of church and world are in a state of collapse, according to the authors; and the goal of Christian Reconstructionism is to "inflict enormous damage" against their enemies.[4]

The second force at large in the world—side by side with Christian Reconstructionism—is God himself. God is not only proving Christian Reconstructionism right by inflicting AIDS upon the world, according to the authors; God is doing nothing less than *plowing up the modern world.* God is destroying the world's optimism; creating wars; unbalancing bud-gets; forcing public education into even further decline; all because God is on the side of Christian Reconstructionism, and must prove them right against their opponents, both ecclesiastical and humanist. There is there-fore not only no neutral ground between Christian and non-Christian; there is no neutral ground between Christian Reconstructionism and the mainstream of confessional Christianity. God has already chosen sides, and is making his will known through his acts of judgment against church and world; that is the Christian Reconstructionist view.

3. Ibid., xiv.
4. Ibid., xxi.

North and DeMar do more than simply gather together the threads of our previous authors; they make a distinct contribution of their own to the set of four leading concepts which ultimately constitutes Christian Reconstructionism. We have called their notion "Christian political domination," and in order to understand what is meant we need to think carefully through several components of their presentation. The first of these is their understanding of the kingdom of God.

According to these authors, the whole notion of the kingdom of God in the Bible is radically misunderstood or misinterpreted in the church at large today. Christians have a "God-given responsibility" to "build" God's kingdom on earth; and that responsibility includes more than simply evangelism or mission, but means specifically a "political kingdom." Building God's kingdom means erasing the traces of Satan's kingdom; erasing the traces of Satan's kingdom necessarily means building God's kingdom, in this world, on this earth. Now, we have seen how Francis Schaeffer expands the Christian mandate to include all culture; every dimension of culture must be rendered "Christian" rather than humanist. There must be Christian art, Christian philosophy, Christian film, Christian schools, Christian economics, Christian government . . . etc. North and DeMar offer what they consider the "simplest and widest" definition possible of God's kingdom, wider even than Schaeffer's notion of culture. Because God rules all creation, God's kingdom is nothing less than a *civilization*. Building the kingdom of God therefore means building a Christian civilization. This cannot and will not happen all at once; but "progressively over time." Christian Reconstructionism will ultimately enact a worldwide Christian civilization, which is God's visible kingdom on earth. Another way of speaking of the same theme is *comprehensive evangelism*; for the gospel to have its true effect, it must shape the whole of civilization, including family, government, church, indeed the entire created order. Repeatedly the authors proclaim: "Christians are required by God to become active in building God's visible kingdom."[5]

What is holding back the church from doing this, according to North and DeMar, is a "secret alliance" between "pietists" within the church and humanists. Pietists are only concerned about the soul at best; or at most about the family, and the church. They balk at the notion of Christian politics. Indeed, it is not only pietists; the whole modern church hates the

5. Ibid., 35.

notion of comprehensive evangelism; hates, that is, the notion that the role of the Christian is to build God's kingdom visibly in the form of a Christian civilization. Humanists also want to keep Christians quiet; and therefore, the "secret alliance" that exists between Christians and humanists leads both to join together in "despising" Christian Reconstructionism.

Now, we need, I think, to examine the Christian Reconstructionist ideas of "building the kingdom of God" and "Christian civilization" a bit more closely in the light of the history of church doctrine. For, according to the authors, Christian Reconstructionists are Calvinists; and the whole notion of building God's Kingdom is the traditional Protestant viewpoint. In fact, a brief examination of church doctrine makes it clear that the facts are otherwise; that the actual historical origin of their concepts—whether they are aware of it or not—is quite different indeed.

For Calvin, the kingdom of God is the mystery of Jesus Christ himself, the true King. Calvin never once, in his exposition of the rule of Christ in the *Institutes*, nor elsewhere, uses the language of "building the kingdom of God." The reasons are not hard to discern: such language is completely absent from the parables of Jesus and the Bible as a whole; and it sounds too much like the late-medieval Pelagianism which Calvin and the major Reformers thoroughly reject, as if human beings "cooperate" with God in the divine mission in the world. No, for Calvin it is Christ alone who builds his kingdom through his sovereign rule over all creation: "For from this we infer its efficacy and benefit for us, as well as its whole force and eternity."[6] The goal of Christ's kingdom is to lift up our hearts and minds to the final glory of his new age; to "await the full fruit of his grace in the age to come."[7] Do Christians now in this world experience triumphant dominion? According to Calvin, that is precisely the misunderstanding of Christ's disciples: "They look for the triumph that comes with warfare accomplished, but Christ urges them to long endurance as if He had said: 'You want to snatch the trophy at the starting-gates, but you must first complete the course. You drag the Kingdom of God to earth, which no-one can achieve unless he first have ascended there into heaven.'"[8] The church, for Calvin, always remains a "pilgrim in this world," in tension between the already and the not-yet, never a "builder

6. Calvin, *Institutes*, 497.

7. Ibid., 498.

8. Calvin, *A Harmony of the Gospels*, 76.

of the kingdom." Not through dominion, but only through tribulation, does the church enter Christ's kingdom; only when the church is low and contemptible on earth does its true beauty shine in the heavens above; only in utter weakness is it truly strong. Thus far, Calvin.

If the language of "building the kingdom" and "Christian civilization" does *not* come from Calvin and classic Protestant dogmatics, then where *does* it come from? Perhaps it is an innovative attempt to speak the language of faith afresh in a new way by Christian Reconstructionists themselves? No, in fact those familiar with the history of doctrine easily recognizes the resonances of the language, which comes from late nineteenth-century Protestant liberalism: from the theology of Albrecht Ritschl in Germany, and from the (derivative) theology of Walter Rauschenbusch in America. Ritschl too wrote endless polemics against pietism, for its failure to take the "this-worldly" task of God's kingdom seriously. Ritschl too wrote of the Kingdom of God as an ethical imperative binding all Christians to "righteous conduct," who must take an "active part" in realizing God's purpose in the world. The sum of the Christian life for Ritschl is "labor for the kingdom of God" (*Reichgottesarbeit*), in which God's kingdom and its righteousness are advanced in the world. In family, law, state, Christian activity is to "gain ground for striving after the kingdom of God."[9] Ultimately the goal of the church is "Christianizing the social order" (the title of one of Rauschenbusch's popular works), or nothing less than "the redemption of society."[10]

Two points need to be made in registering this all-too-obvious link between the language of classic Protestant liberalism and Christian Reconstructionism. First of all, even though the *theological framework* has been borrowed from Protestant liberalism almost wholesale by Christian Reconstructionism, the *political agenda* inserted into that framework is almost the exact opposite. In theology, as in life, extremes sometimes meet. Second of all, it seems fitting to remember that Protestant liberalism in its classic form was decimated in the early twentieth century: first, by the publication in New Testament studies of books by Johannes Weiss and Albert Schweitzer showing that the proclamation of the kingdom of God by Jesus has nothing whatsoever to do with the modern idea of establishing a bourgeois civilization; and perhaps ultimately far

---

9. Ritschl, *Three Essays*, 176.

10. Rauschenbush, *Social Gospel*, 143.

more powerfully, by the devastating experience of the First World War, in which civilized "Christian" nations in Europe all but destroyed one another in the horrors of unending trench warfare. Who could any longer speak so breezily of "building the Kingdom" after Passendale, with 400,000 casualties from the "Christian" nation of Britain, balanced by the loss of 400,000 lives from the "Christian" nation of Germany—only one battle in a war that seemed to gain nothing? Has not history, in its own way, already indeed long since passed severe judgment on the theological framework of "building the kingdom" and "Christian civilization"? Such questions emerged with enormous power in the 1920s in forging a fresh appreciation of Reformation theology in Europe, beginning with Karl Barth's epoch-making commentary on Romans.

Be that as it may, Christian Reconstructionism fills the theological framework of the older Protestant liberalism with a very different political and social content. The major thrust of Christian Reconstructionist effort is named by the adherents "judicial evangelism." How is the message of the Christian faith spread? Traditional Christianity has of course answered very straightforwardly and insistently: by the proclamation of the gospel. Christian Reconstructionism however is convinced that such an answer is narrow-minded. In fact, the message of God's righteousness is also expressed to the world in the form of "political activism," and that of a very particular kind. The goal, let it be remembered, of Christian Reconstructionism, is the establishment of a worldwide Christian civilization, which is equivalent to the visible kingdom of God on earth. This Christian civilization must include "righteous civil government," which communicates to the non-Christian God's redemptive power in history. In sum, Christian Reconstructionism proposes a new "*evangelism through law.*"[11] The entire legal structure of the state—because it is based on God's law in Scripture—is in fact a tool for the evangelism of the world, the spread of Christian civilization everywhere.

Of course this form of so-called political-legal evangelism puts Christian civilization in a head-to-head battle with humanism, according to the authors, a battle now fiercely being waged in our era of humanism. Humanism is a religion; Christian is a religion; and "these two religions are locked in deadly combat."[12] Humanists are trying to "subdue" Christians;

11. North and DeMar, *Christian Reconstructionsim*, 11.
12. Ibid., 39.

and therefore Christianity must "subdue" humanism; no other option is available. Humanists and Christians agree on only two things: that the earth exists, and someone must "own" it; the only question is which of the two will win the battle for "ownership." Unquestionably, according to the authors, the West is already largely totalitarian, including the democracies; so the intensity of the battle is supreme. The rise, for example, of environmentalism in the face of "supposed" ecological problems, and the emergence of a more "unified" Europe, are both profoundly negative signs that the world as a whole is utterly breaking down; that (in the oft-repeated phrase of the authors) *"God is plowing it up"* (italics theirs).

In fact, the opportunity to introduce "legal evangelism" into society—by remaking society according to God's written law—only comes along "about every 250 years."[13] Most Christians go through their entire lives without even the possibility of building God's kingdom on earth through Christian civilization. Christians in our time have a golden opportunity; an opportunity last seen in the American Revolution, so very different from the "satanic" French Revolution. (All of our authors, in various ways—going back to Kuyper—speak in rather venomous tones about the French Revolution, and even about the French generally. I suppose it does need to be pointed out that John Calvin—Jean Cauvin—was a native of France.) The church has been empowered for world dominion, and the world itself must be progressively transformed; the agent of that transformation is not however the gospel, but law, legal evangelism. Christans who deny this simply do not understand the efficacy of biblical law. Biblical law must be applied and carried out by everyone: the civil state, legislators, judges, school teachers, business leaders; only in this way can its true evangelical outreach transform the world. Christian politicians should frame legislation based on the Bible alone as the authority.

In short, the role of biblical law in evangelism is as a tool for dominion. Christian social action, which alone leads to social progress, is based on the evangelical outreach of law. Certainly this is an "original" notion of Christian Reconstructionism. Luther, for example, in his celebrated commentary on Romans, makes abundantly clear the radical distinction between works of the law and faith in the gospel: "Human teachings reveal the righteousness of men, i.e., they teach who is righteous . . . before himself and his fellow men. But only the gospel (*in solo evangelio*) reveals

---

13. Ibid., 52.

the righteousness of God (i.e., who is righteous and how a man can be righteous before God)."[14] For Luther, the gospel is the true treasure of the church, which *alone* puts us right with God; at stake in this radical difference between Christian Reconstructionism and traditional evangelical proclamation is nothing less than the fundamental mission of the church.

Central to the notion of Christian political domination of the world in Christian Reconstructionism is their novel idea of the covenant. While recognizing that classic Protestantism has long labored over the biblical-theological doctrine of the covenant, North and DeMar argue that no one until 1985 was able to "put down on paper precisely what it is, what it involves, and how it works."[15] Needless to say, anyone who has worked through the intense analysis of the biblical and theological concept of the covenant, in even one of the scores and scores of volumes of dogmatics stemming from the reformation, will quickly recognize the astoundingly bold—some would call it arrogant—nature of this remarkable claim. To cite one example among literally hundreds, Francis Turretin, in his locus *De Foedere Gratiae* ("on the covenant of grace") views the theme of the covenant from a dozen different vantage points (*quaestiones*) involving over 100 pages of closely packed text. Examples of this sort could be reproduced endlessly; whole books indeed are devoted simply to the development and elaboration of the Reformed doctrine of the covenant. It is—to say the least—a somewhat surprising claim therefore to hear that only in the late twentieth century has an adequate definition ever been given.

There are, according to the authors, not one but four covenants in the Bible. All four however are funneled through one moment: God's covenant with Adam. It is through Adam that God placed all humanity under the *dominion covenant*. That does not mean that humanity is placed under the sovereign dominion of the Lord, as, for example, Calvin would stress. Rather, God *gives* humanity dominion over all reality. The dominion covenant means *human* dominion over reality. This one dominion covenant actually breaks up into four covenants: a personal covenant with each individual, a covenant with every family, a covenant with the church, and a covenant with the state. The comprehensive reach of the dominion covenant into all areas of life is the point to be stressed: "Christians are

---

14. Luther, *Romans*, 17–18.

15. North and DeMar, *Christian Reconstructionism*, 53.

called by God to exercise dominion in every area of life. God has transferred the ownership of the world to Christians."[16] Christians in fact are called by God to take possession of the world: and that means in family, church, and state. I do think it needs to be observed that what started out as a covenant with humanity (Adam) very quickly (and without real explanation) becomes a covenant with Christians.

Here lies the meaning of the word *reconstruction* in the name of the movement. The goal is nothing less than to "reconstruct" every area of culture and society according to Christian principles by dominion, that is, by taking Christian ownership of the world. That is the fundamental call to discipleship, according to the authors. The exercise by Christians of dominion in the world and all its various social, cultural, and political spheres is identical to the progressive realization of the kingdom of God on earth. Once again, the authors boldly assert that for the first time in the entire history of the Christian church Christian Reconstructionism is offering a biblical alternative to "humanist civilization"; that is, a Christian civilization.

How does their interpretation of Genesis 1:26 compare, say, to Calvin's exegesis? The question is certainly apropos, in light of the authors' repeated assertion that Reconstructionists are Calvinists. Is there a "dominion covenant" in Calvin? "And let them have dominion over the fish of the sea, and over the birds of the air, and over the cattle, and over all the wild animals of the earth, and over every creeping thing that creeps upon the earth"; what does this mean, according to Calvin? First of all, the stress of Calvin is *not* upon a *divine transfer of ownership* to humankind; Calvin's exalted understanding of divine majesty would surely make such a concept outrageous. The stress rather is upon the dignity (*dignitas*) of humankind resulting from the divine care and paternal solicitude (*paterna sollicitudo*). Secondly, the gift of creation is not a task for humanity to complete; rather, it is a divinely accomplished reality to be enjoyed: "Thus man was rich before he was born."[17] Thirdly, the scope of the divine gift is limited to the use of plants and animals for food and life's conveniences, as the biblical text itself indicates; there is no mention in Calvin—here or anywhere—of a comprehensive program of cultural and social domination. God made a beautiful world, fit for humankind to live

---

16. Ibid., 57.

17. Calvin, *Genesis*, 96.

in, and gave humanity its rightful place within that world; for Calvin this is to be a constant source of meditation on the goodness and bounty of God. There is of course no mention of a "covenant" with Adam in Calvin, again for the simple reason that there is no mention of such a covenant in Scripture; the first use of the theme of the covenant in the Old Testament comes only with God's gracious covenant with Noah, and then his stunning new encounter with Abraham.

It is not, I think, fair to say that no one before Christian Reconstructionism was able to offer a satisfying definition of the biblical covenant. Those familiar with the rich literature of Reformation and post-Reformation dogmatics—not to speak of the church fathers and medieval scholasticism—know how wildly inaccurate such a claim truly is. Nor is it accurate to associate the "dominion covenant" with Calvin, or for that matter with Reformed theology generally, as can easily be shown from the sources of that theology. What *is* quite fair to say is that no one before Christian Reconstructionism interpreted the opening chapters of Genesis as a full divine transfer of dominion over all natural *and historical* reality to humankind; and with that transfer the assignment of a task of world domination. "Credit" certainly goes to the authors for this new approach; though putting it to the test theologically is of course another matter.

If, as Christian Reconstructionism proposes, God has transferred ownership of the entire world to Christians, including culture and society; and if with that ownership comes the mandate to Christian political domination of the state worldwide; then what kind of state should be built by Christians as "the kingdom of God on earth"? Through AIDS, and through economic and political turmoil, God is "plowing up the world" to make room for a new Christian state, as Christian Reconstructionists see it; what will that state look like, in this "epoch-making" opportunity of our time? We have already seen that there is no compromise, no neutrality, in respect to "humanism"; *everything* must be "Christian," including science, education, art, film, government, family, law, social, and moral life generally. Christian Reconstructionists utterly reject the pseudo-civilization of "non-believers," including both democracy and communism, and want only to replace it with a comprehensive "Christian civilization." Can we describe this civilization more precisely?

Four elements are essential. First of all, Christian Reconstructionism rejects democracy. Democracies are inherently unstable forms of government, which by definition cannot and will not last: "A democracy places all power in the people. It is a government of the masses. Democratic law is based on the will of the majority . . . a dictatorship normally follows."[18] Instead of democracy, the civil government should be based directly upon the mosaic legislation of the Old Testament. All three branches of government: executive, judicial, and legislative, must base all their decisions upon the written word of the Bible, not the voice of the people. The same is true, of course, for members of families, school administrators, business leaders, and so forth. The government, and indeed the entire society, should operate upon the basis of mosaic legislative "case law."

Second, paradoxically, government should grow and shrink at the same time. When it comes to concern for human welfare, government should shrink dramatically; in fact it should abandon all role in human welfare whatsoever: "Caring for the poor . . . is not the domain of the State."[19] Health care, education, welfare, social security; *none* of these are the responsibility of the state, but belong rather to the family and the church. Taxation should be massively reduced because there would be no public education, no public health care system, no social security, and furthermore, because there should be no restraints whatsoever on personal wealth or the acquisition of wealth. In a "Christian civilization" there is no public education; there are no public hospitals; there is no social security; there is no welfare safety net, no jobless benefits of any kind. All of these are simply eliminated. Nor is there any regulation of business, which largely proceeds according to the model of complete laissez-faire; those who can acquire wealth should be allowed to do so, with no corresponding obligation to the society in which that wealth is acquired. Christian Reconstructionists call this the "minimalist state," and again argue that it is the "biblical" alternative to modern democracy and communism.

Third, on the other hand, at the same time that the state is shrinking—even evaporating—when it comes to concern for the common well-being of society, it is growing dramatically when it comes to intervening in the moral lives of people: "Christian Reconstructionists think civil power should be expanded to bring *negative sanctions against public immorality* [italics theirs]."[20] Hence the paradox; a vanishing state in respect to public welfare, a vastly growing state in respect to moral intervention.

---

18. North and DeMar, *Christian Reconstructionism*, 120–21.

19. Ibid., 92.

20. Ibid., 126.

The scope of this moral intervention is wide indeed: "We need to begin to train ourselves to make a transition: *the transition from humanism's sanctions to the Bible's sanctions, in every area of life.* This includes politics. God has given His people major political responsibilities that they have neglected for at least fifty years, and more than a century. Christians are being challenged by God to reclaim the political realm [italics theirs]."[21] Thus, the power of the state is now to be used in a new direction; no longer for the sake of human welfare, but now for the sake of "sanctions" against immorality. Christians must "impose sanctions" on the world which are drawn from the Bible, not just in politics but in every area of life. In fact, they must call upon God himself to impose his sanctions against all enemies, according to the authors.

What does it mean, fourth, for the new Christian state to impose moral sanctions upon citizens? Rushdoony is of course in the background; the mosaic legislation of the Old Testament—including the penalties imposed against the various "crimes"—should be made the law of the land, every land. Americans now are much too tolerant, according to Christian Reconstructionism; and as a consequence "moral anarchy is battering our nation."[22] In fact, being tolerant is not the true American Way, they argue; toleration is just so much humanist propaganda. People in America have been falsely led to believe that morality is a "personal matter," a view which is a violation of God's law. Above all, they have been conditioned by the humanists to believe that homosexuality (singled out by the authors several times as *the* primary example of moral violation) is a moral choice, not a crime. In a new Christian civilization, homosexuality will be "recriminalized"; it will be against the law to be a homosexual. No homosexual will be allowed to run for office. Because the distinction between a personal moral decision (in the sight of God, *coram Deo*) and a crime is eliminated, the state will indeed have to be expanded considerably for its new role in enforcing "biblical laws" on all citizens of the society, and ultimately the world.

21. Ibid., 52.
22. Ibid., 184.

CHAPTER 5

The Open Proclamation of the Gospel

THUS FAR IN OUR study, we have focused on laying before the reader a detailed study of the four main concepts which constitute Christian Reconstructionism: epistemological dualism, the application of mosaic case law to all society, cultural Christianity, and Christian political domination of the world. Our aim in the first section has been a descriptive analysis of these four concepts. We have drawn each of the four ideas, not from critics of the movement, but from the sources themselves; and not from minor works of little significance, but from the major texts representing the primary ideas of Christian Reconstructionism as a whole. Thus, we now have before us, not the shadow but the substance, not the image but the reality. We have withheld judgment for the sake of clarity.

But in the end, the purpose of our study is not mere clarity, but *decision*: we must decide how the church of Jesus Christ is to respond theologically to the ideas of Christian Reconstructionism. One response would be to debate theologically the various ideas, and offer constructive criticism. Are we not all brothers and sisters in Christ? Do we not all cherish the same faith, and worship the same Lord? I am not however convinced that theological debate would be the faithful response. The other response is to propose that the set of ideas—we are talking about concepts, not people—which constitute Christian Reconstructionism bear so little resemblance to the faith of the gospel, that they must be rejected, not debated. That is, I believe, the necessary response of the church of Jesus Christ to the set of ideas which constitute this movement. As a way of viewing Christianity these ideas so fundamentally distort the gospel as to fall well outside the wide circle of legitimate expression for the language of faith, as defined by sacred Scripture. Not just one of the four ideas, but all of them, misrepresent the very heart of biblical truth.

We begin with epistemological dualism, and set in opposition to it the church's historic commitment to open proclamation of the gospel.

Van Til (and Kuyper before him) divides up the entire world into two, and only two, "systems of truth," one of which is entirely true, the other of which is entirely false. In fact, both go further in dividing humanity itself up into two kinds of people, two kinds of human being, which possess two totally different forms of human consciousness. There are Christian human persons and non-Christian human persons; believer and non-believer; knowers and non-knowers; religious and humanist. And that is it: humanity itself is divided into two forms of human existence along this fault line. We ask: does the gospel of Jesus Christ attested in Holy Scripture divide up the world in this way?

In accordance with Scripture, we do *not* ground our answer to this question by reflecting upon the facts of human consciousness as does Van Til (and Kuyper)—after all, that is the classic position of Protestant liberalism! We ground our answer where the church has always found the answer to its most basic questions of life and death: in the cross of Jesus Christ. And here we find a surprising, even astounding answer. The account of the cross in the Gospel narratives does *not* draw a line between the friends of Jesus on the one side, and the enemies of Jesus on the other. Not at all. A line is drawn, but a very different line indeed. The narrative of Christ's passion is the account of his humiliation, his rejection, his total and complete abandonment. He is rejected by all the religious leaders and authorities: "Then the chief priests and the elders of the people gathered in the palace of the high priest . . . and they conspired to arrest Jesus by stealth and kill him" (Matt 26:3–4). Judas betrays him; the Romans beat and mock him. And then, at the crucial moment when everything is on the line, his own followers flee: "At that hour Jesus said to the crowds, 'Have you come out with swords and clubs to arrest me as though I were a bandit? . . . But all this has taken place, so that the scriptures of the prophets might be fulfilled.' Then all the disciples deserted him and fled" (Matt 26:55–56). Finally even Peter, leader of the apostles, denies him: "Then Peter remembered what Jesus had said: 'Before the cock crows, you will deny me three times.' And he went out and wept bitterly" (Matt 26:75).

Christian Reconstructionism would divide the world between two opposing camps: the Christian and the humanist. The cross of Jesus Christ clearly draws a line of division, but it is a very different line. It is not a line on one side of which the believing friends of Jesus side with him at the cross, while the unbelieving enemies oppose him on the other side. The line of the gospel—as drawn by Scripture itself—quite clearly does not run down in between two kinds of human being. Rather, on the one side of that line is *all humanity*: the pagan Romans, the pious Jews, the confused disciples, the religious authorities, the fickle crowds, the cruel and the cowardly alike. There is no exception; all humanity is there to hand Jesus over to his death. As Paul expresses it: "all have sinned and fall short of the glory of God" (Rom 3:23). And on the other side of that line is the one righteous Man: Jesus himself, who is not only truly human, but also truly divine. The death of Christ—according to the biblical narration of the cross—does not split humanity into knowers and non-knowers; it declares that *all humanity*, religious and irreligious, fails, and fails miserably, to recognize the glory of God in the humiliation of his Son.

And what is the purpose of the dividing line which the Bible draws? According to Christian Reconstrucionism, there is a hostile battle, a struggle, between two ultimately opposing worldviews: the Christian and the humanist. According the Scripture, there is only the one Man Jesus Christ who dies on the cross alone, abandoned by all humanity, pious and impious alike, believing and non-believing alike. The cross does not draw a line which *includes* believers and *excludes* non-believers; the cross draws a line in which Jesus stands alone on the one side, and all humanity is *excluded*, judged as guilty. But why? Jesus himself gives the answer, as he hangs upon the cross in the last moments of his earthly life: "Father, forgive them; for they do not know what they are doing" (Matt 23: 34). The cross of Jesus Christ *excludes* everyone, in order that the love of God in Christ might *include* the whole world. Christ himself takes God's condemnation of the whole world upon himself, and bears it away, bringing it forever to an end: it is finished. All humanity is gathered into the forgiving love of God through the atoning death of Christ for the sins of the world; that is the gospel we cherish, by which we stand or fall. There can be no dividing up of humanity into two ultimate kinds in the light of the cross. There is only one humankind: those for whom Christ died. Christian Reconstructionism stumbles over the offense of the cross.

As followers of Jesus Christ we reject *dualism*; we affirm the *universality* of the gospel.

More is at stake than one single Christological affirmation however; the holistic reading of what the Bible is all about—the very subject matter of Scripture itself—is at issue. According to Van Til—and Christian Reconstructionism after him—the biblical message as a whole is filtered through God's "creation mandate" with Adam. Even the redemptive work of Christ on the cross is to be understood, according to Van Til, in the light of God's relationship to Adam, and through him, to humanity as a whole. God's so-called "covenant" with Adam becomes the central truth of Christian teaching. Is this biblical?

The key passage—which addresses this very issue with exact theological precision—is of course Romans 5:12–21, where Paul sets out a typology between Adam and Christ. There is indeed a relation between the two, according to Paul; but it runs in the exact opposite direction from that set out by Christian Reconstructionism. Yes, sin came through one man, Adam, and grace came through one man, Christ; that is the similarity between these two figures. But Paul immediately makes clear the radical discontinuity between the two: "But the free gift is not like the trespass. For if the many died through the one man's trespass, much more surely have the grace of God and the free gift in the grace of the one man, Jesus Christ, abounded for the many" (v. 15). This "much more surely" makes it abundantly clear that Paul is not in the least establishing a simple balance between Adam and Christ; in fact the radical difference between the two far outweighs the similarity. The only similarity is the universality of the effect: in Adam, all died; in Christ, all are now made alive. But there the similarity ends; there is an "infinite qualitative difference" between Adam and Christ, signaled by the repetitive "much more" throughout the passage. God's free gift of grace in Jesus Christ is different *in kind* from the death which resulted in Adam's sin: "And the free gift is not like the effect of the one man's sin. For the judgment following one trespass brought condemnation, but the free gift following many trespasses brings justification" (v. 16). The infinite qualitative difference of God's free gift of new life in Christ even goes beyond the terrible reality of death which is universal to human experience: "Therefore just as one man's trespass led to condemnation for all, so one man's act of righteousness leads to justification and life for all" (v.17).

Several points need to be drawn out regarding this remarkable and crucial biblical passage. First, the direction of biblical theology—and with it church doctrine—is not from Adam to Christ, as is the case with Christian Reconstructionism. It is exactly the reverse: following Paul, we understand Adam only *in the light of Christ*. Jesus Christ himself—and he alone—is the true subject matter of the witness of Scripture, not a spurious "covenant with Adam." Put in more technical language, we do not move from anthropology to Christology, but the reverse; we move from Christology (our confession of Jesus Christ) to anthropology (our understanding of what it means to be human). Jesus Christ alone tells us what it means to be authentically human. Finding our bearings theologically in a war between two "worldviews" is not a biblical option; we find our bearings by our confession of Christ, and him alone.

Second, *if* it is true, as Paul profoundly asserts, that the free gift of life in Jesus Christ embraces all humanity, literally all human existence; then it is quite clear from Paul's teaching that the reality of Jesus Christ relates *in some way* to every single human being. I do not believe that this passage, or any Pauline passage, openly teaches universal salvation (nor does any Pauline passage *deny* the universal hope of the gospel for that matter); the response of faith is still central for Paul. But it most certainly affirms with absolute clarity that—even apart from the response of faith—Jesus Christ claims every human being upon the earth for himself. Christian Reconstructionism understands Christ in the light of Adam; there is therefore a subset of people within "humanity" which qualify as "belonging to Christ," and an opposing subset which qualify as "not belonging to Christ." But that is not Paul's teaching. Paul understands Adam in the light of Christ. Therefore *all humanity* is in some sense truthfully related to Christ. Again, we are not here raising the issue of salvation by faith, for Paul himself does not raise it in this passage; we *are* pointing out that the essence of being human is defined by, determined by, our relationship to Jesus Christ, as Paul himself insists. Not just "believing" humanity; but all humanity, humanity from Adam, humanity as such, is enclosed within the defining light of Jesus Christ. We must therefore emphatically reject the dualistic notion, which runs throughout Christian Reconstructionism, of two fundamentally different kinds of human being, believing and non-believing. Christ himself makes humanity one by dying for the sins of the whole world; to split them into two is to deny him.

And thirdly, if Christ relates to all humanity—Christian and non-Christian alike—then a basis for dialogue between Christians and non-Christians is established in him. We reject the false alternative of a conservative "holy war" between a Christian worldview and a secular worldview on the one side; and a liberal pluralist notion that dialogue is only possible on the basis that all religious options are equally valid on the other side. No, we confess Jesus Christ, and him alone as Lord of all reality. But following the witness of Scripture, it is precisely that confession which leads us, not to "confrontation" with that which is human as such, but to openness to it. Christ himself became truly human; how can we—precisely as confessing Christians—not embrace the authentically human in our world?

We press further: is Christianity even a worldview at all? According to Van Til (and before him Kuyper, and after him Christian Reconstructionism as a whole), Christianity represents a worldview (among the myriad of other worldviews of human society such as communism, humanism, positivism, existentialism, etc.) in which every single fact in the universe is encapsulated. In knowing the Christian worldview, the believer knows every fact, every single reality that exists, according to its true nature; only the Christian can rightly make this claim. Now we ask: is this the biblical view? And we receive the quite astounding answer: such profound arrogance is condemned not only by the Bible as a whole, but by the figure of God speaking in the Bible in particular. I refer of course to the answer of God to Job (Job 38ff.).

Job's three friends try and fail to meet the challenge of his suffering by offering the traditional wisdom of a theistic "worldview." They are absolutely convinced that within the frameork of a religious worldview about God, an answer to Job's struggles can surely be found. But they fail; and they fail utterly and completely. Truth in the Bible is not understood as correspondence to an absolute or abstract standard (a modern Enlightenment view), but rather as the ability to achieve a desired goal. Job's friends have tried and failed to reach the goal of finding an answer to his suffering, and so are condemned to falsehood. Their theistic worldview—however pious and genuine it may sound—is proven utterly empty and vacuous.

In the end, God himself enters the conversation: "Then the Lord answered Job out of the whirlwind: 'Who is this that darkens counsel by words without knowledge? Gird up your loins like a man, I will question you, and you shall declare to me'" (Job 38:1–3). Human worldviews—even *religious* worldviews—are utterly without understanding in the overpowering light of God's own truth; now it is time for God himself to speak. Two separate divine speeches follow, the double answer serving only to increase the relentless divine rebuke. Above all, over and over again, God attacks—often with terrifying sarcasm—all human pretense to wisdom and understanding, including especially religious pretense.

To those who claim to know the vastness of creation, God responds: "Where were you when I laid the foundation of the earth? Tell me, if you have understanding . . . who laid its cornerstone when the morning stars sang together and all the heavenly beings shouted for joy?" (38:4–7). Again, the crucial point is that God is not attacking a *secular* worldview, but a *religious* worldview, which falsely claims to extend its faith to encompass the entire universe. God continues the attack, not only against those who claim to know the origin of the universe but against those who are ready to explain all phenomena within it: "Have you entered into the springs of the sea, or walked in the recesses of the deep? . . . Have you comprehended the expanse of the earth? Declare, if you know all this" (38:16–18). The massive error of Job's three friends is to assume that a "theistic worldview" is a divine clue which unlocks every mystery in the universe; God sends their vaunted "worldview" crashing to the ground, worthless before his own transcendent majesty. God attacks not only the "knowledge" of their religious worldview, but its capacity for action: "Can you lift up your voice to the clouds, so that a flood of waters may cover you? Can you send forth lightnings, so that they may go and say to you, 'Here we are'?" (38:34–35) What good is their celebrated worldview if it in fact can accomplish nothing, when compared to the omni-competent reality of God? The fact is, their glorious "worldview" cannot even explain the sheer grandeur of a single wild creature, not even the hippopotamus (40:15)! How could it ever become a "system of truth" explaining "every fact in the universe?"

It is essential to catch the radical tone in God's answer to Job and his friends. God's unrelenting attack does not take the form of: "you think you know everything because of your wisdom, your religious worldview, but you really only know a limited amount." God's point—pursued in question after question—is that "you think you know everything, and in fact know *nothing*. You think that faith gives you a 'system of truth' that encompasses every fact in the universe; you fail to realize my *exclusive* claim to wisdom and knowledge in the universe—which I alone have made." In other words, the divine critique is once again qualitative, not quantitative; God is *God*; and for that reason the pretense of any world-view—including a religious one—is utter folly.

Where does that leave Job—and with Job, all of us? Condemned to nothing but ignorance? Not at all. "Then Job answered the Lord: "I know that you can do all things, and that no purpose of yours can be thwarted . . . I had heard of you by the hearing of the ear, but now my eye sees you" (42:1–6). Job has been lifted out of a religious worldview to a living encounter with God. He is no longer talking with his friends *about* God, now he is talking *to* God. John Calvin calls this miraculous new reality the knowledge of God (*cognitio Dei*). By this is not meant a mere noetic process, but a seizing of one's whole life from above in living encounter with God himself; an encounter which transforms heart and mind, will and emotion. Worldviews come and go with practically each news cycle in our global society. The knowledge of God is forever: "Thus says the Lord: Do not let the wise boast in their wisdom, do not let the mighty boast in their might, do not let the wealthy boast in their wealth; but let those who boast boast in this, that they understand and know me, that I am the Lord; I act with steadfast love, justice, and righteousness in the earth, for in these things I delight, says the Lord" (Jer 9:23–24). We turn to Scripture to find the knowledge of God and to grow in that knowledge day by day, until that day when we come fully to know God in his eternal light, who even now already fully knows us.

Van Til (and Kuyper before him) proposes a systemic dualistic contrast between an all-encompassing Christian worldview, and an all-encompassing humanist worldview. Above all, there is *no neutral ground* between these two systemic worldviews, according to Christian Reconstructionism. Every fact in the universe is either a "Christian" fact or a "humanist" fact. (We are surely permitted to ask what constitutes the difference, say, between a "Christian" hydrogen molecule and a "humanist" one.) Van Til in particular sets his epistemological dualism in opposition to the Hodge-Warfield commitment to natural theology, in which a natural capacity for knowing God in all people even after the Fall is upheld. For Van Til, it is either/or; either one affirms the natural theology of Princeton Orthodoxy, or one follows Kuyper into a dualistic battle between two ultimately non-negotiable worldviews. Is this biblical?

As so often happen when it comes to the sharp edges of biblical theology, the apostle Paul provides the crucial response. Where Van Til argues *dualistically* (either/or), Paul always argues *dialectically* (on the one hand . . . yet on the other hand). In the opening chapters of the book of Romans, Paul certainly condemns all natural theology, radically setting aside any natural human capacity for the knowledge of God: "For the wrath of God is revealed from heaven against all ungodliness and wickedness of those who by their wickedness suppress the truth" (Rom 1:18). Paul is not arguing, however, from the point of view of observing two differing forms of human consciousness, the believing and the non-believing, as Van Til/Kuyper do. Paul's argument rather is radically Christological, unfolding solely from the point of view of the revealed gospel, which constitutes the major theme of the entire letter: "For I am not ashamed of the gospel; it is the power of God for salvation to everyone who has faith, to the Jew first and also to the Greek" (1:16). And from the point of view of the gospel—God's revelation in Jesus Christ for the redemption of the world—there is no distinction between the *inability* of irreligious humanity to know God, and the *ability* of religious humanity to know God, between, that is, a believing worldview and an unbelieving worldview. Rather, Paul argues in the light of the gospel that *both* the unbelieving *and* the believing worldview fail, and fail miserably, to know *anything* truthful about God. Paul makes it clear that in so arguing he is advancing no new doctrine, as he makes clear from his quotations from the Psalter: "as it is written: 'There is no one who is righteous, not even one; there is no one who has understanding, there is no one who seeks God. All have turned aside, together they have become worthless; there is no one who shows kindness, there is not even one'" (3:10–12). There is not even one! Certainly not the natural person affirmed by Hodge/Warfield, but neither the religious person brought forward by Van Til/Kuyper. All boasting is excluded, not only the boasting of the non-believer, but also the boasting of the believer: "so that every mouth may be silenced, and the whole world may be held accountable to God" (3:19). Salvation is by faith alone, which is a free gift of the Spirit and not in any sense a human achievement. Faith can never become a human possession, in such a way as to establish an opposition in the world between "religious humanity" and "irreligious humanity" based on human consciousness; that way is completely excluded by the good news of Christ: "Although everyone is a liar, let God be proved true" (3:4); "For there is no distinction, since all have sinned and fall short of the glory of God" (3:23).

That is one side of the dialectic; but Paul does not stop there. Dualisms are always tempting because they are simple; it is black or white, yes or no. Biblical theology is quite clear, but that does not mean that it is obvious; it is at times complex, subtle, multifaceted; and it is essential for church doctrine to follow the rhythms of biblical truth and not force them into the straitjacket of an easy dualism. Does Paul simply condemn all natural thought, all human culture, as utterly worthless, and leave it at that? In the light of the gospel, human culture in no sense whatsoever leads to the knowledge of God; natural theology is utterly foreign to the Bible. But Paul does not simply stop there with one half of the dialectic (on the one hand); as so often he then proceeds to the other side (on the other hand).

A good passage to look at is Philippians 4:8. In this letter, Paul is writing, as it were, his last will and testament to the young congregation in Philippi from a prison cell, while awaiting martyrdom. He knows that his own suffering is a participation in the suffering of Christ. He urges them to continue the life of joyous service to Christ they have embraced, never looking backward, always looking forward. He reminds them to replace anxiety with a life of thankfulness, for God's eternal gift of peace is already present. Then he closes the appeal with our verse: "Finally, beloved, whatever is true, whatever is honorable, whatever is just, whatever is pure, whatever is pleasing, whatever is commendable, if there is any excellence and if there is anything worthy of praise, think about these things." Truth, justice, pleasing (here amiable, or lovely), commendable (here well-spoken of, with a good reputation), moral excellence; these are words of human culture (specifically here, classical Greek culture). Nowhere else in the New Testament does anyone speak of "moral excellence"; the Greek word is used only here; the same is true of the aesthetic word "lovely." These are not words of biblical theology but human culture; yet here they are in Paul's final words in his final letter. Human culture is not redemptive; but nor is it, according to Paul, evil. The cultural world of humanity has a place in the Christian sphere of thought, indeed an important place, given the location of this passage in the letter, and in the Pauline corpus. The same Paul who, on the one hand, can condemn *both* the religious and the irreligious world as utterly worthless, can, on the other hand, maintain that human culture has its modest place as a source of insight for the Christian community. Setting up a dualistic battle between a "Christian worldview" and a "humanist worldview" is a simplistic and serious distortion of the Pauline gospel, a distortion which strikes at the heart of the mystery of grace.

To summarize thus far: the epistemological dualism of Christian Reconstructionism posits (on the basis of phenomenological observation of human consciousness) an absolute contrast between knower and non-knower in matters of Christian faith; the whole world is divided between these two classes of people, and there is no breach in the wall between them. Furthermore, the subject-matter of Scripture is contained within a larger "system of truth" or worldview, which again is set in absolute contrast with the "unbelieving" worldview of humanism (which includes every other worldview except the Christian); every fact in the universe is included within the Christian worldview, or misperceived within the humanist worldview. Moreover, all human culture is to be completely re-jected as "humanist" and therefore false; false in its entirety, without any possible use to the Christian "worldview." Now, we have opposed the epis-temological dualism of Christian Reconstructionism by pointing to the cross of Jesus Christ, which far from drawing a line of division between knower and non-knower, first *excludes* (as sinner), in order to *include* (as redeemed sinner), all humanity. We have argued that the subject matter of Scripture is Jesus Christ himself, not a larger philosophical "system of truth"; and that the knowledge of God in Scripture shatters any and every worldview, even especially a religious one. We have observed the Pauline dialectical approach to culture: which utterly rejects culture along with all human religious experience as a source for the knowledge of God, but which embraces culture as a *relative* source of insight and value for the Christian community.

We conclude our response to the epistemological dualism of Christian Reconstructionism by pointing out that it is not new. Already in the second century, the church was struggling to define and defend the faith of the gospel; and one of the primary opponents was gnosticism. The first great theologian of the church, Irenaeus, wrote his magnum opus *Against All Heresies* largely in order to articulate the church's defense of the gospel against the gnostic threat, which posed a fundamental mis-understanding of the true reality of Jesus Christ according to Scripture. The gnostics, too, split the world up into knowers (spiritual) and non-knowers (carnal), and of course declared that only true gnostics belong to the class of spiritual beings. Irenaeus comments: "they run us down

. . . as utterly contemptible and ignorant persons, while they highly exalt themselves, and claim to be perfect, and the elect seed."[1] The gnostics, too, insist on a self-enclosed religious worldview, which only those who have "knowledge" can rightly understand. Again, Irenaeus insists: "You see, my friend, the method which these men employ to deceive themselves, while they abuse the Scriptures by endeavoring to support their own system out of them."[2] Even the very meaning of words can only be determined, not by normal use, but by their function within the gnostic system. Irenaeus counters: "Thus it is that, wresting from the truth every one of the expressions which have been cited, and taking a bad advantage of the names, they have transferred them to their own system."[3]

Against gnosticism, Irenaeus is unyielding, and opposes the public and open preaching of the gospel of Jesus Christ. The gospel is not for knowers as opposed to non-knowers; the gospel is sent forth unto the whole world: "But as the sun, that creature of God, is one and the same throughout the whole world, so also the preaching of the truth shineth everywhere, and enlightens all men that are willing to come to a knowledge of the truth."[4] The gospel cannot and must not be encapsulated within a worldview or "system of truth," but must be measured by the inner coherence of the subject matter of Scripture itself: "Such then, is their system, which neither the prophets announced, nor the Lord taught, nor the apostles delivered, but of which they boast that beyond all others they have a perfect knowledge. They gather their views from other sources than Scriptures . . . In doing so, however, they disregard the order and the connection of the Scriptures, and so far as in them lies, dismember and destroy the truth."[5] The reading of the Scriptures is not a private exercise of the "knowers," but a public affirmation of God's universal truth: "Since, therefore, the entire Scriptures, the prophets, and the Gospels, can be clearly, unambiguously, and harmoniously understood by all, although all do not believe them . . . those persons will seem truly foolish who blind

1. Irenaeus, *Ante-Nicene Fathers*, 1, 324.
2. Ibid., 329.
3. Ibid.
4. Ibid., 331.
5. Ibid., 326.

their eyes to such a clear demonstration, and will not behold the light of the announcement made to them."[6]

Our point of course is not to argue an exact correspondence between Christian Reconstructionism and gnosticism; our point rather is that the *same epistemological dualism* which first appeared in the one now appears in the other, with equally disastrous theological results. I think it is highly significant that *preaching the Word* is scarcely even mentioned by Van Til, or by any of the Christian Reconstructionists after him. What is the mission of the church if not the open proclamation of the gospel to all humanity: "And Jesus said to them, 'Go into all the world and proclaim the good news to the whole creation'" (Mark 16:15)? What is our one hope, but that the *universal* knowledge of God will embrace the whole creation: "They will not hurt or destroy on all my holy mountain; for the earth will be full of the knowledge of the Lord as the waters cover the sea" (Isa 11:9)? By this hope the church of Jesus Christ stands or falls; and by the radiant light of this hope, *all* "worldviews," religious and non-religious, are but the lingering shadow of a mist which evaporates into thin air.

6. Ibid., 398.

CHAPTER 6

Law and Gospel

W HAT KIND OF A world would result if Rushdoony's "mosaic legislation" were applied in all the societies of the world?

Democracy of course would be abolished along with communism;
and although those with minor religious doctrinal errors could survive,
serious opponents of Christianity would be liquidated. There would not be
a Federal Church in the United States; but there would be a State Church
of Florida, a State Church of Alabama, a State Church of Montana, and so
forth; all sponsored by a required poll tax on all citizens. The idea of equal
opportunity for all would be legally abolished; some people after all are
"created" inferior, and simply must learn to live with their "subordinate"
status, according to Rushdoony. The government will shut down all agencies that have anything whatsoever to do with the general health and welfare of the people: social security, Medicare, Medicaid, cancer research,
Alzheimer's research, food stamps, unemployment insurance, all will
cease. People in need of a helping hand must rely exclusively upon their
own families; and if that doesn't work, then local congregations must supply the difference. Thus, families and local churches must carry out the
advanced medical research, the economic safety net, the social support of
the elderly, once carried out by the body politic. *If* anyone ever turns to
the government for help, they automatically lose their citizenship, including their right to vote. Publicly supported universities and hospitals will
shut down; all public education will end. *Fathers and mothers* will now
train the next generation of particle physicists, microbiologists, literary
critics, neurologists, brain surgeons, linguists, international diplomats,

oceanographers, specialists in sustainable architecture, and wildlife managers. *Local congregations* will run the health care system, and train the surgeons, nurses, administrative staff, anesthesiologists, as well as designing and building the next generation of advanced medical equipment; and at the same time, they will make sure that no more organ transplants ever again take place.

Armed Citizen Councils will police the neighborhoods, looking for adulterers, homosexuals, and prostitutes; these will be turned over to the government to be put to death. There will be no prisons to hold them in, so justice will be swift. Presumably, given the exponential rise in mass executions, there will be needed a new government agency, a State Execution Authority, which will doubtless give full employment to the economy given the massive number of new hires required. Cases will be decided by judges trained in religious education schools based on the Bible, and decisions will be suggested by the local pastor of each judge. With the shutdown of all public institutions of higher learning, the law school as we know it will cease to exist; lawyers will no longer be trained in the precise traditions of American jurisprudence, but in religious instruction. Racial, cultural, interracial marriages will be frowned upon by society at large; friendship with homosexuals (those that are still alive) will be banned; men will be expected to be "men," and women will be expected to be "women," as defined by clear rules of dominance and submission. For those who stray too far from biblical teaching: the death penalty. Ballet, opera, symphony orchestras, art galleries; shut down for the "heathen" temples they are. We may never know exactly what we are eating; there will be no regulation of the food industry. We may never know what drugs we are ingesting; there will be no regulation of the pharmaceutical industry. You may or may not consume contaminated beef; you may or may not get your prescribed medicine, a placebo, or a dangerous narcotic; and since your butcher and pharmacist are home-schooled in their field, the chances are high that mistakes will be made. Unions will be banned; any form of job discrimination will be perfectly legal, whether on the basis of gender, race, creed; for the "fact" is God did not create everyone equal. Sexual orientation is not an issue anyway, since the "homosexual problem" will be handled a different way. Your surgeon will be home-schooled in the latest techniques of surgical procedure, or at best educated at church; the judge before whom you must appear in court will be trained in the finest traditions of religious instruction according to the State Religion. Young people who lose their way in life for a while will certainly have no chance to find it again; juvenile delinquents will be put to death. (Obviously, the story of the Prodigal Son will need to be carefully rewritten, or least reedited, in the new Bibles produced by the home-schooled printers). According to Rushdoony, Native Americans are non-Christians, and are hence not real Americans. (The real Americans are the Christians who came and stole the land from the Native Americans.) Each man will be proud of his "property," which includes his land, his home, his wife, his children; and the role of the state is to protect a man's property at all costs. Reverence for life will be abolished as a humanist lie; the whole society will inculcate one primary virtue, which is domination. Christians will be lent money at no interest; non-Christians will be charged interest. Parents who lean too far to the liberal side politically must be abandoned by their children; the emotionalism of "love," as Rushdoony defines it, has no place in the new order. Indeed, if anyone sins, not only their sins, but they themselves, must be hated by everyone; unconditional love is forbidden by state law. Those who chafe at this new order will be whipped by the lash forty times; if they balk too often and too loudly, they will be handed over to the State Execution Authority. "God will cleanse the land."

How are we to respond to the new law-order of Christian Reconstructionism? We could certainly call it Medieval, but that would be a gross injustice . . . to the Middle Ages. After all, the medieval period witnessed the rise of the great universities at Paris, Oxford, Cambridge (now scorned by Rushdoony as "humanist seedbeds of rebellion" and shut down in the age of "Reconstruction"). The Middle Ages also produced the lovely and intricate music of Machaut and Perotin (now ignored by concert halls closed forever). Medieval culture beheld the glory of Dante and Chaucer (banned of course from public libraries, that no longer exist anyway under Rushdoony's "law-structure"). We could compare it to the early Christian heresy of "Jewish Christianity," but that is certainty unfair . . . to the early Jewish Christians, who at least retained a living connection with the Jewish synagogue at a time when the rest of Christianity was falling into the trap of believing that Christianity had simply superceded Judaism in the divine economy (which runs counter to the clear teaching of Paul in Romans 9–11). By contrast, Rushdoony shows no interest in—and certainly no credible knowledge of—rabbinic Judaism and its approach to Torah whatsoever. We could compare it to early Puritanism, but that would again be quite unfair . . . to the Puritans, many of whom fought vigorously for religious freedom, after suffering the lethal blows of European monarchies.

No, in fact I do not believe this barbaric new world order needs any special condemnation from me. As a religious ideology of bitter anger and fanaticism, it is filled with such malice, ignorance, bigotry, prejudice, and toxic hatred of the human race that it clearly stands self-condemned.

What I propose to do instead in this chapter is to trace a brief series of lines of biblical interpretation, in order to demonstrate that Scripture, according to its own inner theological coherence, points in a decisively different direction from Christian Reconstructionism, both as a whole, and in detail. The Bible is *not* a legal codex written for judges; the Bible is the Word of God, written and shaped according to God's gracious purpose for the instruction of the church and the world. Five concerns need to be addressed.

The *first* is the context of divine Law within the Old Testament itself. According to Rushdoony, the laws of the Bible contain legal "principles" which are given as the content of God's "law covenant" and are valid for all nations at all times. The clear testimony of the Old Testament runs in the opposite direction of these major assumptions of Rushdoony.

There are no legal or moral "principles" in the Old Testament, or anywhere in the Bible for that matter; the whole notion of such "principles" was an invention of nineteenth-century biblical criticism based in German idealism, now completely discredited by modern biblical scholarship. The Bible contains God's *commandments*, not moral principles; God's commands are always concrete, specific, and immediate, and call only for the response of wholehearted obedience. To Abraham, God commands: "Go from your country and your kindred and your father's house . . ." (Gen 12:1). To Jacob, God commands: "Return to your country and to your kindred, and I will do you good" (Gen 32:9). There is no "law system" or "law order" in the Bible; there is the living reality of God, and his sovereign revealed will. Any attempt to bypass the active revelation of God in his commandments through a "system" of laws seeks to pull the divine will down into human hands: "Ah, you make iniquitous decrees, who write oppressive statutes, to turn aside the needy from justice and to rob the poor of my people of their right" (Isa 10:1–2). God's will is *God's* will; it can never become a convenient platform for human legal or ethical speculation. God in the Old Testament is a living person who freely communicates his will. There is no place in the Bible for translating legal principles into specific cases (casuistry) through rational reflection. God is the living Lord who even now continues actively to communicate his will to the church and the world through the medium of Scripture by his Spirit. Right behavior is a *response* to a living Person who commands, *not* conformity to an abstract closed legal system.

Furthermore, covenant and law are not simply folded into each other, as two sides of the same coin. According to the Old Testament, there is a clear order, as laid out in the prologue of the Ten Commandments: "I am the Lord your God who brought you out of the land of Egypt, out of the house of slavery" (Exod 20:2). The prologue makes it abundantly clear: everything, which now unfolds as an expression of the divine will, follows from the fact that God has *already* delivered Israel from bondage. God has already made himself known as the Redeemer of his people by grace alone; his authority to claim his people is based on his gracious redeeming act of love. His covenant is a covenant of grace. Therefore, Israel does not somehow become the people of God by obeying the commandments, a complete misconstrual of the biblical dynamic. Israel *already is* God's people because he has chosen them in the mystery of his electing love: "It was not because you were more numerous than any other people that the Lord set his heart on you and chose you—for you were the fewest of all peoples. It was because the Lord loved you" (Deut 7:7). The covenant with Israel is a covenant of free unmerited grace, based solely on the electing love of God according to his own sovereign and mysterious initiative and purpose. The law is given not to *establish* them as the people of God, but to show them the necessary *response* of gratitude to God's grace; obedience to the law does *not* make them the people of God. According to the clear witness of the Old Testament, the covenant of grace is the basis of law; law is not the basis of the covenant.

Moreover, while God's will according to the Old Testament is a coherent whole, which can be summarized and faithfully applied, it is also crucial to observe the *time-conditioned* quality of the divine command. The conquest of the land by violent assault under Joshua provides a good example. Despite the command not to kill, God tells the Israelites to destroy the inhabitants of Canaan when they take possession of the land (Book of Joshua). Clearly Rushdoony wants to extend the wholesale slaughter of "infidels" ("cleansing the land") as a legal "principle" into the present, as he makes it clear repeatedly throughout his book; the whole generation of "hippies" needs so to be "cleansed." So we need to ask whether his approach is warranted by the book of Joshua. Of course, the easy way out would be to suggest that Israel simply misunderstood God under Joshua's leadership; that they *thought* they were doing God's will by destroying the Canaanites, but they in fact misheard God's Word. While some modernist commentaries pursue this line, they do so only by setting the book of Joshua in a theological context alien to the theological shape of Scripture itself; there is no evidence whatsoever in the Bible that the conquest was a mistake. Israel was doing what God commanded. But Scripture also makes it clear that what Israel did—as terrible as it is to modern readers—was to be done once, and once only; never again was the conquest of the land by violence to be repeated. The conquest was a one-time only event in the divine purpose; and God's command therefore was *time-conditioned*, and not a general principle. The best illustration of this comes when the prophets speak of a return to the land, the same land which Joshua led the people into by conquest. They not only avoid all talk of conquest by violence; they *reverse* rather than sustain the tradition of a holy war: "In days to come the mountain of the Lord's house shall be established as the highest of the mountains . . . He shall judge between the nations, and shall arbitrate for many peoples; they shall beat their swords into plowshares, and their spears into pruning hooks; nation shall not lift up sword against nation, neither shall they learn war any more" (Isa 2:1–4). The point is not that Isaiah is criticizing the conquest tradition; the point is that *God himself* is consigning conquest of the holy land by violence to a time now forever in the past. The way forward in the Promised Land is now and forever the way of peace.

The *second* line of biblical interpretation concerns the charge of "antinomianism" which Rushdoony makes against the whole of historic mainstream Christianity in all its manifestations. As we have seen, Rushdoony's idiosyncratic definition of antinomianism is "a rejection of the judicial law of the Old Testament as a blueprint for society"; no other major or minor theologian in the history of the church defines antinomianism this way, which ordinarily means the attempt to cut Christian life free from any obligation to the moral life (the Ten Commandments). For example Polanus, in his *Syntagma Theologiae Christianae*, first lists nine reasons why the Christian community must retain the Decalogue as a guide for Christian life, and then offers his opposing arguments against the Antinomians (*Antinomi*), who "deny that that the Decalogue pertains to Christians."[1] Why, then, did the church *not* follow Rushdoony; why from the very beginning did the church refuse to enforce the judicial laws of the Old Testament as a civil code, drawing the line at the Ten Commandments instead?

It needs to be carefully observed and stressed—even within the confines of the Old Testament witness itself—that the Ten Commandments are set apart from the rest of the Law of God given to Moses on Mount Sinai, a fact both Jewish and Christian traditions have long pointed out. Only the Ten Commandments are spoken directly by God: "Then God spoke all these words: I am the Lord your God" (Exod 20:1–2); the rest of the divine law is given to the people through the voice of Moses. Unlike the remaining laws, the Ten Commandments are comprehensive ("Do not steal"), and yet at the same time entirely concrete. They are not addressed to particular groups within Israel, such as the priests, or the Levites; but to the people of Israel as a whole, without qualification. The Ten Commandments are clearly positioned at the beginning of the entire mosaic law, not simply as an introduction, but as a summary of the full content of the divine will. There are no appeals to inner motivation in the Ten Commandments; they are simply to be obeyed because they are God's will. They are given a special name: literally the Ten Words (Deut 4:13), and written on two tablets of stone. When God finishes delivering them, there is a definitive break: "These words the Lord spoke with a loud voice to your whole assembly at the mountain out of the fire, the cloud, and the thick darkness, and he added no more" (Deut 5:22). Turning to the New Testament, when asked to summarize the divine rule for life, Jesus himself simply repeats the commandments of the Decalogue to the rich young ruler (Matt 19:16–23). For all of these reasons, the church universal, then and now, recognizes a distinction between the Ten Commandments and the rest of the law of Moses. Despite the complex dialectic of law and gospel, there is an affirmation of the role of the Ten Commandments in the Christian life (the "third use of the law"), a rejection of which is perceived as antinomianism (being "against the law"). Thus, the historic Christian affirmation of the special role of the Ten Commandments both in Scripture and in the life of the church and society is grounded in the theological shape of Scripture itself. Rushdoony is wrong to insist on an "all or nothing" approach to mosaic law; the very shape of Scripture itself

---

1. Polanus, *Syntagma*, 2267.

warrants a quite different approach, as the church has recognized from the beginning.

Why did the universal church begin and continue to stress the continuing validity of the Ten Commandments (the moral law), while affirming the divine *origin* but not the continuing divine *claim* of the remaining legislation (the judicial and ceremonial law)? Why didn't Christians in fact do what Rushdoony wants them now to do: wherever they go to insist that societies order themselves according to the judicial laws of the Old Testament? Were they simply being unfaithful, as Rushdoony suggests? The answers lie in a solemn meeting—the *apostolic conference*—which took place in the apostolic church, as recorded in Acts 15. The background of the chapter is the astonishing growth of the Word in the mission of the gospel to the nations. The first Christians were practicing Jews; but now because of the mission to the Gentiles by the apostle Paul, the church was seeing large converts among non-Jews. The foreground of the letter is the issue of circumcision, required by the judicial law of Moses. Jewish Christians of course were already circumcised; should Gentile converts to Christianity be required to be circumcised? Must a person go through the judicial law of Moses in order to arrive at the gospel of Jesus Christ? Some of the Jewish Christians want to argue that observing the judicial law of Moses is required for salvation: "Then certain individuals came down from Judea and were teaching the brothers, 'Unless you are circumcised according to the custom of Moses, you cannot be saved'" (Acts 15:1). Others simply wanted Gentiles who had already converted to Christ to become circumcised, as a sign of obedience: "But some believers who belonged to the sect of the Pharisees stood up and said, 'It is necessary for them to be circumcised and ordered to keep the law of Moses'" (15:5). The *apostolic conference* has been called to settle the issue (thus setting the pattern for later church councils). Peter makes it clear that in giving them the Holy Spirit, God has absolutely confirmed once and for all the salvation of the Gentiles. Should they—the Gentiles—be required to keep the law, when even the Jews have failed: "Now therefore why are you putting God to the test by placing on the neck of the disciples a yoke that neither our ancestors nor we have been able to bear?" (v.10). His conclusion is definitive; both Jew and non-Jew are saved apart from the law by the grace of Christ: "On the contrary, we believe that we will be saved through the grace of the Lord Jesus Christ, just as they will" (v. 11). Thus, both the way of entrance into salvation, and the subsequent mode of life which flows from that salvation, are by the grace of Christ alone: apart from obedience to the law of Moses. The whole council agrees; and seals their agreement by a pragmatic declaration designed to insure unity: "Therefore I have reached the decision that we should not trouble those Gentiles who are turning to God, but we should write to them to abstain only from things polluted by idols, and from fornication, and whatever has been strangled by blood" (v. 19). This is conciliatory advice, to promote unity; the issue of free grace is settled.

So, why did not church universal, almost from the beginning of the post-apostolic period, as if by reflex make a distinction between the moral law on the one hand, and the ceremonial/judicial law on the other; accepting the continuing validity of the former for the Christian life (within the covenant of grace), but not the latter? The church universal was—and is—following a sacred decision made by the apostolic church in the light of the conversion of the Gentiles. It *has* to be insisted, in the light of a Jewish and Gentile church, that salvation is by faith alone apart from works of the law; and that the manner of Christian life is by grace alone apart from law. Both justification and sanctification are by grace, not law; that is the essence of Peter's point. When the church isolated the Ten Commandments as uniquely relevant to the Christian life, they were maybe not following the *letter* of Acts 15, which offers only a minimal list of suggested requirements; they were however following the *spirit* of Acts 15, in offering to the church and the world those dimensions of Old Testament Law which remain the eternal expression of God's will for church and society.

The *third* line of biblical interpretation comes from the apostle Paul, and is focused upon his vigorous attack against the Judaizers in the book of Galatians. According to Rushdoony, two theological principles underline his "mosaic" law-system: we are justified by grace, but sanctified by law; and we, as Christians, are bound to the legal system of Moses, including circumcision. How do these two principles stand up to Paul's fierce and vehement attack against his opponents?

In the book of Galatians—unlike the situation in Acts 15—it is already accepted that even Gentiles can believe the gospel, receive the Spirit, and inherit the eternal promise of God. That is no longer considered an issue by Paul's opponents. The question now is rather this: once the Gentiles, the non-Jews, believe in Christ, are they required to accept the authority of the law of Moses, and to fulfill its requirements? Paul's strategy in the letter is to argue that in fact *both* questions are ultimately the same question; that those who truly understand that salvation is by grace through faith alone, must necessarily also realize that Christian obedience unfolds under the gracious guidance of the Spirit, *not* in fulfillment of works of the law. You cannot start with grace, and proceed back to law; that is the fatal error of the Judaizers. Those who fully realize the stunning reality of God's free grace in Jesus Christ also *must* realize that grace alone continues to guide the life of obedience from beginning to end; a return to the law is nothing short of "a different gospel" (Gal 1:6).

The free grace of the gospel comes apart from works of the law: "We ourselves are Jews by birth and not Gentile sinners; yet we know that a person is justified not by the works of the law but through faith in Jesus Christ" (2:15). But then, should Christians, having come to justification through faith alone, be sanctified by law? Paul answers: "But if I build up again the very things that I once tore down, then I demonstrate that I am a transgressor. For through the law I died to the law, so that I might live to God . . . And the life I now live in the flesh I live by faith in the Son of God" (2:18–20). For Paul, if *sanctification* does not come by sheer grace alone, then *justification* itself is utterly lost. To begin with justification by grace, and then to proceed to sanctification by law, is to deny everything: "You foolish Galatians! . . . Did you receive the Spirit by doing the works of the law or by believing what you heard? Are you so foolish? Having started with the Spirit, are you now ending with the flesh? . . . does God supply you with the Spirit and work miracles among you by your doing the works of the law, or by your believing what you heard?" (3:1–5). As Paul makes clear throughout the letter, to misunderstand the nature of sanctification, is inevitably to misunderstand justification as well; and that is to misunderstand everything. Calvin calls justification and sanctification a twofold *grace* (*duplex gratia*); they are not to be separated, nor can they simply be fused, but above all both flow from grace alone, not law.

Even more is at stake for Paul: and that is the fundamental *freedom* of the Christian, which come as a gracious gift of Christ. The rigorous demand of the Judaizers that the Gentile Christian fulfill the letter of the mosaic legislation now that they have believed not only shows a fatal misunderstanding of the grace of God in both justifying and sanctifying grace; it also robs the Christian of the freedom for which Christ himself died: "For freedom Christ has set us free. Stand firm, therefore, and do not submit again to a yoke of slavery" (5:1). The Judaizers insist that Gentile

Christians follow the Jewish tradition of the law, as symbolized by the rite of circumcision. Paul has already made the point that such insistence fails to recognize the truth of God's grace; he now stresses that it also steals away the joyous freedom of the gospel: "Listen! I, Paul, am telling you that if you let yourselves be circumcised Christ will be of no benefit to you . . . For you were called to freedom" (5:2, 13). Falling back into rigid legalism by becoming circumcised—as a sign of embracing mosaic legislation—is to lose everything that matters: "For neither circumcision nor uncircumcision is anything; but a new creation is everything!" (6:15). Against Rushdoony and Christian Reconstructionism, we must insist with perfect clarity: Christian life is a new creation by the Spirit; it is most emphatically not a sanctification by law.

The *fourth* line of biblical interpretation—and here we enter into the true heart of the matter—concerns the absolute, sovereign, active authority of the risen and exalted Christ, by whose authority alone the truth of Scripture is rightly understood and judged. We have already seen that Jesus affirms the Old Testament law, by repeating the Ten Commandments when asked for the true way of eternal life (Matt 19:16ff.). God's will is made known in his concrete commandments—not in ethical principles, nor in a "law-system"—in the New Testament as well as the Old. Jesus affirms the commandments of the Old Testament; yet he does so in the absolute freedom of the true Giver of those commandments. We do not understand Jesus in the light of Old Testament law; we understand Old Testament law only in the light of the one true Lawgiver, which is Christ the Lord. A good example—which predominates throughout the gospel narratives—is the radically new interpretation Jesus gives of the Sabbath command. Jesus does not treat the Sabbath command as a moral principle, locked within a legal system, subject to a variety of case-law nuances of application. With sheer freedom, Jesus at the same time embraces the Sabbath command, yet radically reverses its true purpose and function: "The Sabbath was made for man, not man for the Sabbath" (Mark 2:27). The Sabbath is not a day of moral obligation and onerous burden; the Sabbath is a festival of joy, a gift of God to be received with gratitude and blessing. When confronted with the "case law" of healing on the Sabbath, Jesus announces the new age of God's rule, which brings wholeness to life, not death (Mark 3:1–6).

Nor can the interpretation be sustained which argues that Jesus is simply undercutting the Pharisaical understanding of the Old Testament, but leaving the Old Testament itself intact. The entire Old Testament cultic apparatus of distinction between clean and unclean foods—which Rushdoony maintains is still in force for Christians, including the avoidance of eating catfish!—is overturned by Jesus on the grounds of a radically new interpretation of evil. It is not what a person eats that makes them evil; it is what comes out from the human heart. The Gospel of Mark makes a side-comment to the reader to make it crystal clear how pervasive this rejection of Old Testament food laws has to be seen: "Thus he declared all foods clean" (Mark 7:19). The authority of Christ over the law extends not only to the Pharisees, but into the heart of the Old Testament as well. To summarize thus far: the New Testament affirmation of Old Testament law is certain, but it is also complex. Jesus himself alone is the one true Interpreter of the law. At times, his affirmation comes in the form of reversing the traditional theological understanding of a commandment; at other times, his affirmation distinguishes the true will of God (all foods clean) from its Old Testament written manifestation (clean and unclean foods).

Of course, the radical reinterpretation of the divine law given by Jesus is most evident and perhaps most familiar from the Sermon on the Mount. In a series of six antitheses (You have heard that it was said . . . but I say unto you), Jesus speaks with sovereign authority grounded only in his own person. He does not give any ethical or legal principles; he does not offer any case laws; he affirms the divine law, but once again radicalizes it by confronting the listener with the genuine purpose of God's will. Case law, piety, law-systems; all are cast aside as worthless subterfuges and evasions in the light of the true intent of God's own word. For example, the issue of adultery cannot be formulated in terms of a legal principle and a set of cases; rather, the true matter of adultery extends to the heart: "You have heard that it was said, 'You shall not commit adultery.' But I say to you that everyone who looks at a woman with lust has already committed adultery in his heart" (Matt 5:27–28). Again, the command not to kill is affirmed, but the true intent digs deep into the inner life of human emotion, forbidding even the angry thought or word (5:21–26). Love does not extend just to members of the community of faith, or to family—the common way of the heathen—but reaches out even to the enemy (5:43–48). The true will of God engages and claims the whole person: intellect, emotions, and will, and breaks completely free of any form of "law-system": "The eye is the lamp of the body. So, if your eye is healthy, your whole body will be full of light; but if your eye is unhealthy, your whole body will be full of darkness" (6:22–23). In sum, Jesus alone defines the will of God as made known in the law. Jesus does *not* bring a new law (*nova lex*); rather, he establishes the eternal revealed law of God by determining with sovereign authority (I say to you) its true meaning. Any interpretation of biblical law—such as Rushdoony's—which simply bypasses the basic Christological foundation of God's revealed will misses the point entirely not only of the New Testament, but also of the Old: "No one sews a piece of unshrunk cloth on an old cloak; otherwise, the patch pulls away from it, the new from the old, and a worse tear is made. And no one puts new wine into old wineskins; otherwise, the wine will burst the skins, and the wine is lost, and so are the skins; but one puts new wine into fresh wineskins" (Mark 2:21–22).

Calvin makes the essential Christological basis of biblical interpretation of God's law crystal clear. It is crucial, argues Calvin, when approaching the Ten Commandments, to recognize that the laws are to be measured in accordance to the purpose of the Lawgiver, not the reverse. We cannot bend God to our understanding of legal principles; we must be conformed in our understanding to the sovereign divine intent, which alone matters: "Let us agree that through the law man's life is molded not only to outward honesty but to inward and spiritual righteousness. Although no one can deny this, very few duly note it. This happens because they do not look to the Lawgiver, by whose character the nature of the law also is to be appraised."[2] Thus, according to Calvin, we do not learn the character of God by examining the principles and cases of a closed legal system; exactly the opposite, we learn the true meaning of the biblical laws by measuring them against the character of the living reality of God himself. And who is the God of whom we speak? For Calvin (as for the Reformers generally), there can be only one answer: "When we say that this is the meaning of the law, we are not thrusting forward a new interpretation of our own, but we are following Christ, its best interpreter."[3] Jesus Christ alone is the true Interpreter of the law. Calvin's point is not a narrow biblicistic one; that each time an interpretation of an Old Testament law is given, one ought to check the New Testament to see if Jesus in his earthly life makes a comment upon it. For Calvin, the *whole*

2. Calvin, *Institutes*, 372.
3. Ibid., 373.

of Scripture points to the ultimate, absolute authority of the risen Christ; and every single word of the Bible—including the law of God—is rightly understood only in the light of Christ's sovereign and gracious rule. The same point is carried over into the second generation of the Reformation by Ursinus: "Christ is the substance and ground of the entire Scriptures" (*Totius Scripturae summa & fundamentum est Christus*).[4]

Our fifth and final line of biblical interpretation presses home what must necessarily be another basis for our categorical rejection of Christian Reconstruction. According to Rushdoony, the function of the biblical "law-system" is to carry out God's "dominion covenant" with Adam; a covenant with humankind to dominate the earth in God's place, and to set up a hierarchy of dominion in social and family relations ("some people are simply born to a lower status," "wives are a form of property," etc.). We have already pointed out that the entire basis of Christian Reconstructionism—the "covenant with Adam"—is a biblical fiction; as anyone with a good concordance can easily determine, God makes no covenant whatsoever with Adam. But now it is time to address the central, core issue: is "dominion" the key to biblical law? We have already established that any answer to this question has to be grounded in the authority of Christ the Lord; he alone determines the true meaning of God's Law, for he alone is the true embodiment of God's will for the church and the world. Does Jesus ever answer the question: what is the true meaning of God's Law?

"When the Pharisees heard that Jesus had silenced the Sadducees, they gathered together, and one of them, a lawyer, asked him a question to test him. 'Teacher, which commandment in the law is the greatest?'" We do not have to guess; despite the dubious motives of the questioner, the very issue we now have before us is posed to Jesus with the utmost urgency, leaving no room for equivocation. Rabbinic interpretation largely avoided an answer to the question of a central focus of the commandments: all the commandments of God carry the same weight, because they are all commandments of God. Christian Reconstructionism, according to Rushdoony, has already given *its* answer: the greatest commandment is to exercise dominion over the earth: all other commandments find their true meaning according to this "creation mandate." Jesus answers quite differently indeed: "He said to him, 'You shall love the Lord your

---

4. Ursinus, *Commentary*, 3.

God with all your heart and with all you soul, and with all your mind.' This is the greatest and first commandment. And a second is like it: 'You shall love your neighbor as yourself.' On these two commandments hang all the law and the prophets" (Matt 22:34). As a door hangs on its two hinges, so not only the Law but also the Prophets hand on the twofold command of love for God with one's whole being, and love for neighbor as oneself. According to Christ, the twofold rule of love is the true meaning of God's law—not any abstract principle of dominion. The neighbor is not only the fellow believer, but even the enemy (Luke 10:29ff.); there can be no boundaries to love, no conditions imposed upon God's absolute imperative of radical love which embraces the stranger, the foreigner, the outcast, the sinner, the prostitute. Love for neighbor is always expressed in the concrete practice of mercy and kindness. In sum: God's revealed will is not a closed legal system of principles and cases, which are all to be blindly followed as isolated parts of a comprehensive "law structure"; God's will requires a total response of one's whole existence, focused on love for God with complete abandon, and concrete love for neighbor without condition or restriction: this is "much more important that all whole burnt offerings and sacrifices" (Mark 12:33).

The historic Christian church heard the twofold rule of love exactly as it is intended in the canonical form of Scripture: neither as an alternative to the Law, nor as a mere summation of the law, but rather as a guiding light for the true interpretation of the law according to the living will of God in Christ. In his brilliant treatise on biblical interpretation, *On Christian Doctrine*, Augustine wrestles with the question of knowing when to take the words of the Bible as literal or figurative expressions. The church of Jesus Christ is not left without direction; it is given a method when clarity of understanding is crucial: "And generally this method consists in this: that whatever appears in the divine Word that does not literally pertain to virtuous behavior . . . you must take to be figurative. Virtuous behavior pertains to the love of God and of one's neighbor."[5] When there is confusion in the church concerning the proper theological context for understanding a passage of Scripture, the twofold rule of love is the final court of appeal. If it does not lead to greater love for God or neighbor, somehow it has gone terribly wrong; if it leads to love for God and neighbor, the right path has at last been found.

5. Augustine, *Christian Doctrine*, 87–88.

CHAPTER 7

The Call to Global Mission

WE WILL LET THE classic Reformed theology professed in the *Westminster Confession of Faith* (1648)—widely regarded as the definitive statement of orthodoxy for English speaking Reformed Christian doctrine—have the last word in our response to Rushdoony's position, and the first word in our response to Schaeffer's. After defining the Ten Commandments as the moral law, which "perpetually binds" everyone as a "perfect rule of righteousness," the Confession then adds: "Besides this law, commonly called moral, God was pleased to give to the people of Israel . . . ceremonial laws. All which ceremonial laws are now abrogated under the New Testament. To them also . . . he gave sundry judicial laws, which expired together with the state of that people, not obliging any now, further than the general equity thereof may require."[1] As we have seen, the Confession is putting its seal to a division within the mosaic law ultimately going back to the New Testament church itself, and reflected throughout the mainstream of the ecumenical church. *No* part of the law of Moses is considered anything less than the Word of God written; the question is rather the continuing applicability of certain parts under the divine economy. The *whole* law of Moses points infallibly to the eternal will of God; but each part is governed in different ways by the active purpose of God for the church and the world. The church today is wise, in my judgment, to remain within this broad consensus, and not to return to a new legalism which leads nowhere.

---

1. Pelikan and Hotchkiss, *Creeds and Confessions,* II, 629.

The Confession makes a further point, which opens the fresh topic of the present chapter: "Good works are only such as God hath commanded in his holy Word, and not such as, without the warrant thereof, are devised by men out of blind zeal, or upon pretense of good intention."[2] Fanatical religious zeal and fine intentions are no substitute for the concrete command of God's Word. In our language today, good causes—whether on the religious right or on the religious left makes no difference—only distort the witness of the gospel when turned by pious extremism away from the revealed will of God, no matter how well-intended those causes may be.

The "good cause" of Francis Schaeffer—and the Christian Reconstrutionism which follows him—is easily summarized. Christianity and Western culture are two sides of the same coin. The truth of the Christian "worldview" is expressed in Western culture; while the foundation of Western culture is the truth of the Christian "worldview." The two—Christianity and the West—stand or fall together, and though western culture means Europe and America, Schaeffer clearly focuses almost exclusively upon the United States. Until a century ago—so his version of events runs—Christianity and western culture proceeded hand in hand relatively unimpeded. But suddenly, around the time of the early twentieth century, the linkage between Christianity and Western culture came under attack by secular humanism. The primary, indeed the supreme task of current Christian activity, is to defend at all costs the unity of Christianity and Western culture against attack by secular humanism: hence the "Christian Manifesto." If things get really bad—as they almost certainly will and perhaps already are, according to Schaeffer—then violence against the state—the government of the United States—is not only warranted but necessary. Thus, Schaeffer.

Before we proceed to our response to the cultural Christianity of Schaeffer, we need to quickly remind ourselves of a point already made in the response to Van Til: which is that the gospel of Jesus Christ is not a worldview. The gospel which the Christian church professes, by which it stands or falls, is not a worldview, but a *name*: Jesus Christ is the gospel, and the gospel is Jesus Christ. A worldview did not die on the cross for the sins of the world, and rise again on third day; Jesus Christ and he alone is God's gracious gift of redemptive love for all humankind. A worldview

2. Ibid., II, 625.

does not call us each by name before the foundation of the world, nor hold us in the palms of his hands; Jesus Christ is the true reality of God's electing love who knows us better than we know ourselves, who is nearer than we are to ourselves, who loves us in ways of which we may never be fully aware. A worldview did not create, nor does it rule the universe; in fact no worldview ever created a single substance in all reality. All things came into being through him, who alone commands the heavens and the earth, and rules the cosmos according to his mysterious good pleasure. All reality is not moving toward the final day of the revealing of a world-view; but instead moving toward the final day of the return of Christ the Lord, whom every eye will see, and before whom every knee will bow. Worldviews—all worldviews, including religious, even Christian ones— are idols; they have no eyes to see, no ears to hear: "See, they are like stubble, the fire consumes them; they cannot deliver themselves from the power of the flame" (Isa 47:14). Only the living reality of God in Jesus Christ is the truth of Christian faith: "Turn to me and be saved, all the ends of the earth! For I am God, and there is no other" (Isa 45: 22).

We are now in a position to take a further step and ask: is the link between Christianity and Western culture, which Christian Reconstructionism both presupposes and defends, a biblical option? Granted that the biblical canon often shows great flexibility on a variety of issues; is this an issue within the realm of legitimate articulation of the language of faith? Or does cultural Christianity cross a scripturally deter-mined line? That is, does it overstep a boundary of faith beyond which the gospel is not rightly understood or proclaimed? I am convinced that the latter is the case.

First of all, the gospel of Jesus Christ does not adopt or confirm the moral values of the world; it overturns them. The new world of God al-ready made real in the advent of Christ does not underscore and endorse the social, political, and cultural values of human moral life; it radically reverses them. The world celebrates and embraces "traditional moral values," passed along from generation to generation, focused on the past ("You have heard that it was said to those of ancient times"); the word of Jesus Christ not only calls those values into question, but utterly rejects them with sovereign authority grounded in the majesty of his own person ("But I say to you . . .") and always points to the eternal future ("your kingdom come . . ."). The gospel shakes the very foundations of moral cul-ture, calling for radical love without limits, even love for enemies. Culture celebrates the "successful" person, the self-made individual whom others want to emulate. Not so the gospel of Jesus Christ, which offers the ultimate divine blessing to the poor in spirit, to those who mourn, to the meek, to the merciful, to the peacemakers. The world of culture highlights the self-promoter, the ambitious, the self-affirming achiever. The gospel of Jesus Christ by sharp contrast confers the blessing of God's eternal kingdom on those who are despised by the "inner circle": "Blessed are those who are persecuted for righteousness' sake, for theirs is the kingdom of heaven" (Matt 5:10). The world of culture loves prosperity, and holds up as a model for its citizens those who have through hard work and self-achievement gained the fortune which they rightly deserved. The gospel says: "No one can serve two masters; for a slave will either hate the one and love the other, or be devoted to the one and despise the other. You cannot serve God and wealth" (Matt 6:24). The world of human moral values defines security in terms of wealth, and wealth in terms of security. The gospel says to the rich fool who lives by the illusion of security: "This very night your life is being demanded of you. And the things you have prepared, whose will they be?" (Luke 12:21) The world of culture holds up the wealthy and successful as models of upward mobility; and the poor and needy as those who must work harder to find the success they need to "get to where they ought to be." The gospel of Jesus Christ turns this moral equation quite literally upside down: "Let the believer who is lowly boast in being raised up, and the rich in being brought low, because the rich will disappear like a flower in the field" (Jas 1:9). Indeed, the wealthy and successful are most to be pitied, for they stand under the coming judgment of God: "Come now, you rich people, weep and wail for the miseries that are coming to you. Your riches have rotted, and your clothes are moth-eaten. Your gold and silver have rusted, and their rust will be evidence against you . . . Listen! The wages of the laborers who mowed your fields . . . and the cries of the harvesters have reached the ears of the Lord of hosts" (Jas 5:1–6).

The sole criterion of truth according to Scripture is the cross of Jesus Christ. In the world of human culture there is self-promotion, self-achievement, self-sufficiency; all are destroyed by the sovereign and effective power of the cross: "But God chose what is foolish in the world to shame the wise; God chose what is weak in the world to shame the strong; God chose what is low and despised in the world, things that are not, to reduce to nothing things that are, so that no one might boast in the presence of God" (1 Cor 1:27–29). Mere nothings, total nobodies, complete outsiders; these are embraced by God's love in the cross, putting to shame the self-exalted folly of the so-called "somebodies" of culture and society, the movers and shakers of the world. God in Christ becomes nothing, that the nothings of the world might become truly something in him. The world of culture celebrates the "insider"; the gospel draws all who follow Christ "outside the camp," there to suffer with him (Heb 13:13). The world of culture is proud of moral striving, moral achievement, moral excellence; the gospel comes, not to the morally superior, but to the broken, the hurting, the wounded, the struggling: "And as he sat at dinner in Levi's house, many tax collectors and sinners were also sitting with Jesus and his disciples—for there were many who followed him. When the scribes of the Pharisees saw that he was eating with sinners and tax collectors, they said to his disciples, 'Why does he eat with tax collectors and sinners?' When Jesus heard this, he said to them, 'Those who are well have no need of a physician, but those who are sick; I have come to call not the righteous but sinners'" (Mark 2:15–17). The world of culture applauds the strong individual, who stands on one's own two feet apart from and above the rest; the gospel of Jesus Christ, by sharp contrast, says: "Indeed, the body does not consist of one member but of many . . . the eye cannot say to the hand, "I have no need of you" . . . On the contrary, the members of the body that seem to be weaker are indispensable" (1 Cor 12:14–26). The world of culture loves the successful winner: the gospel of Jesus Christ says, the first shall be last, and the last shall be first. The world of culture focuses on what is *achieved*; the gospel of Jesus Christ proclaims only what is *received*. The gospel is God's sovereign word of grace, which cannot be linked to *any* cultural, political, social, personal, or national agenda: "We have renounced disgraceful, underhanded ways; we refuse to practice cunning or to tamper with God's Word . . . For what we preach is not ourselves, but Jesus Christ as Lord" (2 Cor 4:1–5).

Cultural Christianity is certainly under attack; but the real threat does not come from secular humanism, which is mere child's-play. The real attack on cultural Christianity—the only one which comes with eternal power and force, which cannot be ignored or denied—is the attack which comes from the gospel itself: "Then you will begin to say, 'We ate and drank with you, and you taught in our streets.' But he will say, 'I do not know where you come from; go away from me, all evildoers!' . . . Then people will come from east and west, from north and south, and will eat in the kingdom of God. Indeed, some are last who will be first, and some are first who will be last" (Matt 13:22–29).

Second of all, the very fact that the gospel overturns the moral values of *all* human culture, makes it clear and certain that the same gospel is not in any way tied to any *one form* of human culture. At stake here is nothing less than the fundamental call of Christ to mission. In the "great commission" passage of Matthew's Gospel (28:16–20), Christ the risen and exalted Lord now addresses his disciples in Galilee, where they have come to meet him. His authority now extends throughout the entire cosmos; all earthly powers and peoples now serve the absolute, unconditioned sovereignty of his rule over all that exists. The language of the passage is clear: the unrestricted rule of Christ over all nations and peoples is not an event which still lies in the future, but is even now a present reality ("All authority . . . has been given . . ."). Until now, the earthly ministry of Christ was restricted to Israel (10:5); now the restriction is lifted, and the new and stunning universal mission of the disciples is derived from the ultimate authority of Christ over all peoples: "Go therefore and make disciples of all nations." The eternal presence of Christ with his missionary community is the sole guarantee of their fruitfulness, the sole source of their complete confidence. Thus, the church's global mission is grounded Christologically, not geopolitically. Christ does not call the disciples to spread the Christian religion far and wide throughout the earth, as if to complete a process of religious growth simply begun in his own earthly ministry but left unfulfilled in the end. The authority of Christ over all nations, all races, all tribes, all peoples, all cultures, is *already a fulfilled reality*; and it is that very reality which forms the *basis*, not the *goal*, of Christian mission. Christians are not called to extend Christ's rule—how could we possibly do what he has already done!?—but in the light of that universal rule, to carry the gospel to the ends of the earth. The presence of Christ alone is the true source and power of our global mission.

The book of Acts of course carries the account of that mission forward. Once again, something inconceivably new breaks forth into the community of faith, and through them, to the surrounding world: the presence of the Holy Spirit. The Spirit comes on Pentecost. The call of Christ to proclaim the gospel to the ends of the earth is now supported by a new gift of the Spirit to the small gathered community of faith: which is the gift of language, the ability to speak the same gospel, yet in the different known languages of the surrounding peoples and cultures. Suddenly, the promise is immediately and miraculously realized; the gospel is no longer believed by Jews only, but by Gentiles from various cultural regions all across the Roman empire: "Amazed and astonished, they asked, 'Are not all these who are speaking Galileans? And how is it that we hear, each of us, in our own native language? Parthians, Medes, Elamites, and residents of Mesopotamia, Judea and Cappadocia, Pontus and Asia, Phrygia and Pamphylia, Egypt and the part of Libya belonging to Cyrene, and visitors from Rome, both Jews and proselytes, Cretans and Arabs—in our own language we hear them speaking'" (Acts 2:5–13). Once again, the book of Acts—no more than the call to mission in Matthew—has nothing to do with a history of the rise of the Christian religion. Having given the Spirit to the apostles on Pentecost, the first thing that Peter does is preach the Word of God (2:14–36). The history which follows is a *history of the Word of God*, which is made effective by the power of the Spirit. The universal spread of the Word is the crucial subject-matter of the book of Acts: "But the word of God continued to advance and gain adherents" (12:24). The preached Word is nothing less than the means through which the full power of the risen and exalted Christ is present, through the activity of the Spirit. The ascended Lord appears directly only to Paul on the road to Damascus; Christ is present to all others through the proclaimed word, which is shaped into a message with a discernible form and content, as the many sermons in the book of Acts show.

Now, the question is bound to arise at some decisive moment: does the gospel now being proclaimed truly break free of the boundaries of culture? Does the gospel of Jesus Christ, the Jew of Nazareth, really and truly apply to all nations and peoples? That moment comes in Acts 10, when God himself commands Peter to speak the good news to Cornelius, a Gentile Roman officer. At first Peter resists the very idea of carrying the gospel from Jew to Gentile: "By no means, Lord." God's own voice overrules Peter's false piety: "What God has made clean, you must not call profane" (10:9–16). The decisive moment comes when the Spirit falls on "all who heard the word" (10:44), thus providing the indisputable sign that the Gentiles—the nations—have now received their share in God's promise to Israel. Cornelius and his household are baptized; the gospel has crossed a border from which it will never recede. And while the event itself is startling and new, it is the same Peter who on Pentecost made it fully clear that the promise to the nations is grounded firmly in the Old

Testament witness itself: "Then everyone who calls on the name of the Lord shall be saved" (Acts 2:21, Peter quoting the prophet Joel).

To summarize: the call to mission of the risen Christ is a universal call. The coming of the Spirit on Pentecost confirms that call by the gift of language, the ability to speak the message across linguistic and cultural divisions. Peter, the Jew, is himself called to take the decisive step: to make the first Gentile convert. Even Peter at first resists, and only God's own intervention overcomes his resistance. Then, the home church at Jerusalem also resists; but Peter's persuasive voice wins the day (Acts 15). The gospel *cannot* be locked into one language, one culture, one nation, one people, one race, one tribe; the gospel by definition thrusts itself across cultural borders, breaks down linguistic fences and national barriers, and reaches ever outward to the global community. Once again, the notion of a western cultural Christianity as proposed by Christian Reconstructionism falls to the ground before the majesty of the risen Christ, who sends forth his disciples to the whole creation.

Now, in my judgment—and I am certainly not alone—we are at the present time in an *exactly* analogous situation to that of the early church. Then, the Word broke free from the original cultural locus which it addressed, and spread in the power of the Spirit across the earth. We are now in our very own time witnessing a similar revolution in the shape of global Christianity. First some facts (gathered from the recent and authoritative summary, *The World's Christians,* by Douglas Jacobsen, with extensive bibliographies region by region), before we draw the analogy more explicitly.

Only a few decades ago, there was talk of explosive growth in what was then called the "third world" of Christianity. That so-called third world—which includes Christians in Latin America, Africa, and Asia—is now in fact the *first world* in global Christianity; while traditional Western Christianity in Europe and North America is certainly now in Christian terms the new *third world*. The stunning and miraculous changes have happened so fast that describing them, according to Jacobsen, is like "trying to catch a train as it is pulling away from the station."[3] The trajectory which began in the early church as a movement from Hebrew to the surrounding Greco-Roman culture, moving into Persian, Indian, Arabic, Berber, Gothic, and Coptic cultural domains, is even now coming

3. Jacobsen, *World's Christians*, xiii.

to fruition in the brilliant new reality of the global Christian community. We can do no more here than provide a few samples from the amazing new landscape of faith.

At the present time, 13 percent of the world's Christian live in North America; while 15 percent live in Western Europe. By contrast, 24 percent live in Latin America, 20 percent live in Sub-Saharan Africa, and 14 percent live in East, Central, and South Asia. There are thus more Asian Christians than American Christians. There are almost as many Christians in Latin America alone as there are in North America and Western Europe *combined*. These incredible facts reflect staggering growth in global Christianity that has taken place only in the last few decades, often hardly reported in the mainstream Western press, and scarcely observed or recognized among even educated church people in the western context. At the turn of the twentieth century, there were around 7 million Christians in all of Africa, 5 percent of the African population. Today there are over 400 million Christians in Africa, which make up over half of the total African population. At the turn of the century, only 2 percent of the world's Christians lived in Africa; today, one out of every five Christians living in the world is African. More than half of all Anglicans live in Africa; a quarter—one out of every four Anglicans—live in Nigeria alone. Again, Christians were only a tiny minority in South Korea in the early twentieth century. Today, nearly a third of all South Koreans are Christian. There are more Presbyterians in South Korea than in the United States! Again, one out of every four Christians in the world today lives in Latin America. The growth of Christianity in Latin America over the last decades has not been gradual, but exponential. Much of the Christianity in the global South—Africa and Latin America—is traditional in doctrine, and Scripturally based.

It is *not* the case that the explosive growth of global Christianity simply represents a colonial export of *Western* Christianity to the rest of the world. I make this statement not only on an empirical basis (based on the assessment of the experts in the field), but more importantly a theological one. We remember from the book of Acts: the history of the church is not the history of the institutional church, but the *history of the Word*, which acts in the power of the Spirit to cross every barrier of culture, nation, and race. What is spreading across the face of the earth is not western Christianity, but the *living Word of God*. In fact, it is better to speak, not of a geographical shift in the center of Christianity from the west to the south; but rather, to speak of a new recognition that *there is no geographical center* to Christianity. Christianity is not Western, and never was. According to Scripture, we have to think *Christologically*, not geographically. The global church is now, and always has been, centered in the risen and exalted Lord, Jesus Christ: "There is one body and one Spirit, just as you were called to the one hope of your calling, one Lord, one faith, one baptism, one God and Father of all, who is above all and through all and in all" (Eph 4:4–6).

Let us now return to our original analogy. We are in fact living through an extraordinary time for the Christian community of faith. Perhaps at no other time in the long history of the church of Jesus Christ has the fundamental call to mission, and the basic promise of the gospel, been more dramatically realized than in the present time. We are lucky to be alive in this amazing time; to share with our brothers and sisters around the globe the advent of a genuinely global Christian community, centered only in the risen Lord. So I ask: is this the appropriate time to insist—as Schaeffer surely does—that Christianity is Western, and the West is Christian? I believe the answer is once again self-evident; a Western cultural Christianity is exactly the *wrong* message to bring to the world. I am convinced that the idea of Western cultural Christianity was *never* consistent with the gospel. But most certainly, it is doubly wrong now, when the entire world is celebrating a new time of global mission: "O sing to the Lord a new song; sing to the Lord, all the earth. Sing to the Lord, bless his name; tell of his salvation from day to day. Declare his glory among the nations, his marvelous works among all the peoples" (Ps 96:1–3). Indeed: among *all peoples*. The early church witnessed the spread of the gospel beyond Palestine to the lands beyond. Resistance was powerful by the "home church," but it was overcome. So, in our time, resistance to global Christianity in the shape of idealizing a western cultural Christianity has to be unmasked and overcome by a new openness to the movement of God's Word and Spirit in and throughout the world.

A final line of biblical, theological, and moral interpretation must conclude our response to Schaeffer's position. In the final chapters of his book—clearly as a *crescendo* in his overall argument and not as an afterthought—the theme of using force against the government by Christians is accented. He is clearly talking about the government of the United States (though of course Schaeffer spent most of his adult life in Switzerland). He argues that force may very well be necessary against the government of the United States of America, if and when it adopts positions which he considers contrary to Christian interests. With deeply disturbing ambiguity, he leaves no guidelines for the application of such force, or the conditions under which it should be applied; only the clear and open statement that its necessity is becoming increasingly apparent for Christians. How are we to respond?

The classic passage in the Bible for the religiously motivated use of force against the state—and the profoundly ambivalent moral implications involved—is of course the narrative of the slaying of the Egyptian by Moses (Exod 2:11–25). Moses—before his call by God—sees his fellow Hebrews enslaved and mistreated by the Egyptians. One day, he watches as an Egyptian beats a Hebrew, in fact one of his own relatives. Moses quickly glances around in all directions, and seeing no witness, kills that Egyptian overseer, burying his lifeless body in the sand. The very next day he sees two fellow Hebrews fighting with one another. He asks the offending party in the fight why he is striking his fellow Hebrew. The man replies that Moses has no right to act as ruler and chief over anybody; and then taunts him: "do you mean to kill me as you killed the Egyptian?" Moses suddenly realizes that the murder of the previous day had not been accomplished unobserved. Pharaoh himself finds out; and Moses flees for his life. Only then, in a new time, and in a new way, does Moses receive a new call from God as deliverer of the people.

Several features of this remarkable passage are noteworthy, and address the religious use of violence for social justice quite directly. Certainly the passage itself nowhere condemns the *motive* of Moses; it simply reports the action with the implicit assumption that Moses is acting for the sake of compassion for his people. But the *deed* of Moses sets in motion a terrible chain of unintended consequences which have nothing to do with his original motive, however good it might have been. Moses clearly thought that he was acting for the right reason, and that his fellow Hebrews would quickly recognize his true purpose. Yet his deed of killing the Egyptian, and his attempt to reconcile the two struggling Hebrews, implies a claim to personal authority that no one else is prepared to recognize. "Who made you ruler over us" asks the Hebrew fighting his neighbor. As if to say: "You have taken the life of another human being; now you are going to call my behavior into question? Exactly who made you the judge of all things mortal?" The Hebrew accuses Moses of wanting to kill him also, which is of course untrue; but the point is that

Moses has left himself open to just such an accusation by the nature of his action in killing the Egyptian, regardless of the honesty of motive. Moses thought he was becoming a leader; only to realize that he had become a threat, to his own people! Again, the story exposes the ambiguous feature of Moses' attempt to kill the Egyptian in secret. He thinks no one observes the murder, carefully looking "this way and that"; and when it is over, he gets rid of the evidence of his action. Yet, the text clearly leaves open the realization that a hidden deed under these circumstances is simply impossible. The truth is bound to come out. Moses thought he was doing the right thing for his people, and ends up fleeing the country in disgrace: rejected by the state and by his own people, just one more political terrorist. Finally, the text leaves the reader to ponder a terrible anomaly. Moses—however pure his motives—has taken the life of another human being. When he then intervenes in the fight between the two men with the challenge: "Why do you strike your fellow Hebrew?" his role as reconciler of enemies is seriously undermined by his own act of violence, committed only the day before. How can a killer one day, suddenly become a peacemaker the next?

In my judgment, Schaeffer's call to use force against the United States must be firmly rejected. There is the issue of *context*: in a world of religiously motivated violence run amuck such as our contemporary world, what possible meaning could such Christian violence have but yet another act of religious extremism, indistinguishable from all others, which are abhorred by the Christian community and the world at large? Have we not had enough religious violence in our world; what possible good could come of more? Violence in the name of Western Christian civilization is neither Christian nor civilized. There is the issue of *historical judgment*: Schaeffer's comparison of the contemporary government of the United States of America with the relation between England and colonial America is frankly absurd. The early colonists came to the new world seeking a religious freedom they could not find in the old. Didn't we come to the new world tired of being told by the state what to do and believe? England was (at that time) a tyrannical power bent on oppressing the American colonies against their own interests, and against their will. The United States of America is a *democracy*, indeed, a democracy which, some of us believe—despite its flaws—continues to offer the world a shining beacon of hope. Over its history, Christians have joined their fellow citizens in pledging their highest honor to *defend* this democracy; and so many have made good on that pledge on sacred battlefields the world over. The very suggestion that *Christians* should be entertaining the notion of using force against the government of the United States—because it refuses to bend to their "dominion" and enforce a so-called "Christian" regime upon the people—is, simply, unworthy of the gospel we cherish, and the Lord whom we serve. Our confession is not: "Christians rule!" Our confession is: *Christ is Lord*!

CHAPTER 8

The Call to Discipleship

T HE VIEWS OF GARY North and Gary DeMar in their book *Christian Reconstructionism: What It is, What It Isn't* have already been analyzed in detail in a previous chapter. They can be summarized here as follows. God has made a "covenant of dominion" with humanity in which he has transferred ownership of the world to humankind. That covenant has been partially realized through the Kingdom of God brought by Jesus, which is a new Christian civilization to be built further and extended everywhere by Christians in all realms of society. Christian dominion over all life is defined by Christian Reconstructionism as the kingdom of God on earth. It is to be carried out through the means of "evangelism through law," which involves using law as a vehicle for spreading the influence of Christian civilization and therefore gaining Christian adherents. The call to discipleship is—so it is argued—the call to Christian dominion over the world.

I do not believe these ideas need further explication; they are clear enough as outlined by the authors, and as summarized for our purposes in the chapter presenting their views. Nor do I propose a theological debate on biblical grounds of the relative merits of their views, suggesting strengths and weaknesses. For, despite occasional citations of biblical passages here and there, the authors have taken snippets of Scriptural truth so out of their theological context within the inner theological coherence of the biblical message as a whole, that debate is not possible. Both Irenaeus and Tertullian once made the same argument in their rejection of the heresy of gnosticism, when they appealed to the rule of faith (*regula fidei*). The rule of faith is not identical to the written word, but nor is it separated from it; the rule of faith is the inner logic of the subject-matter of Scripture. Inside the rule of faith, there is plenty of room for debate on a vast variety of theological topics. But such, according to Irenaeus and Tertullian, is not the case with gnosticism, which has ignored the rule of faith found in Scripture. Instead, gnosticism is pursuing its own political and personal agenda with Scripture as a convenient tool. As Irenaeus puts it, the gnostics have taken the true image portrayed in Scripture, which is Christ the King, and rearranged the elements in the picture, turning it into a perverse and corrupt counter-image: "By transferring passages, and dressing them up anew, and making one thing out of another, they succeed in deluding many . . . just as if one, when a beautiful image of a king has been constructed by a skillful artist . . . should then take this image all to pieces, should rearrange the gems, and so fit them together as to make them in the form of a dog . . . and even that poorly executed."[1] Tertullian, tired of the misuse of Scripture for purposes foreign to its theological content, states confidently: "To know nothing in opposition to the rule of faith is to know all things."[2] When dealing with false doctrine, according to Tertullian, it is no longer a question of the meaning of individual "proof-texts" here and there; the meaning of Scripture as a whole is at stake. In such a case, there is only the church's resounding No, for the sake of the utter clarity and beauty of the glorious Yes of the gospel. Such will be my argument against the views of the present authors, unfolding along four central points at issue.

The first point at issue is their contention that God "transfers ownership of the earth" to humankind in a "dominion covenant" or "creation mandate." Their astounding claim is based on a single verse from the Bible, Genesis 1:26. We have already shown that the idea of a "covenant" is simply absent from the passage altogether; the notion that a divine covenant with Adam provides the major theological framework for the rest of Scripture is a fiction of the authors, certainly not a truth of the Bible. God's one covenant of grace made real in Jesus Christ provides the genuine theological framework of the Bible; Jesus Christ himself is the "eternal covenant" which alone gives us peace with God and makes us complete in all things (Heb 13:20–21). Moreover, as we saw in the profound exegesis of John Calvin in his extensive commentary on Genesis, God does not

---

1. Irenaeus, *Ante-Nicene Fathers*, 1, 326.
2. Tertullian, *Ante-Nicene Fathers*, 3, 250.

offer the sheer beauty of creation to humanity as a project to be completed, but as a gift to be enjoyed. Dominion in the Bible does not mean going out to complete something that God has only started; it means receiving with thanksgiving the abundant goodness God has *already* provided in all its fullness. Again, the portrait of paradise in Genesis is one of *harmony*; harmony between God and humankind, harmony between humankind and the natural world, and harmony between one human being and another. The relation of humanity to the natural world, as Wollebius rightly observes, was "mild and peaceful."[3] It is that biblical *picture* which defines the "rule" which humanity is to follow in the natural world, not a pre-established *meaning* of the term—invented by the authors—which is then allowed to ride roughshod over the clear biblical picture. Finally, there is no "creation mandate" in the Bible for the simple reason that humankind is not in any sense the Creator; God alone is the Creator of the heavens and the earth. The Hebrew word for the act of creation in the opening chapters of Genesis is a technical term describing an act of creation with no preexisting material reality (*creatio ex nihilo*), and therefore an act bearing no analogy whatsoever to any human act of creation. Put simply: only God creates, in the Bible, never humanity; that is the message of Genesis 1–3. Creation comes to its completion: "Thus the heavens and the earth were finished, and all their multitude" (Gen 2:1). The seventh and final day of creation is a day of divine rest; and, it is crucial to observe, God invites humankind to share in the divine *rest* (the Sabbath), not in the divine *work* of creation. In sum, from the point of view of Genesis 1–3 the notion that "God transfers ownership of the world to humanity" is not only groundless, but contradicted by the plain sense of the passage. *God* is the Creator, and God alone.

If we look elsewhere in the Bible, the rejection of such a notion only becomes all the more clear. The constant refrain throughout the whole of Scripture is resounding: "The earth is the Lord's and all that is in it, the world, and those who live in" (Ps 24:1). The earth is the Lord's, not ours; that is the radiant teaching of the Bible. God never in any sense whatsoever transfers ownership of his creation to humanity; for God, and God alone, is *God*. How can we possibly speak of a "transfer of ownership" in the face of him who declares: "For every wild animal of the forest is mine, the cattle on a thousand hills. I know all the birds of the air, and all that moves

---

3. Wollebius, *Compendium*, 66.

in the field is mine. If I were hungry, I would not tell you, for the world and all that is in it is mine" (Ps 50:10–12)? Is this how a God speaks who has "transferred ownership of the world to humanity?" Or is this a God who speaks from the sovereign and exclusive power of his own creative rule, which cannot in any way be shared with another? Indeed, not only does God *not* transfer ownership of the world to humanity; God shows no interest in *any partnership* with humankind at all: "Who has measured the waters in the hollow of his hand and marked off the heavens with a span, enclosed the dust of the earth in a measure, and weighed the mountains in scales and the hills in a balance? Who has directed the spirit of the Lord, or as his counselor has instructed him?" (Isa 40:12–13). The form of disputation in this passage is rhetorical; the answer is *obvious*, that no one works as co-creator with God. Even the slightest hint of an analogy with human forms of creativity is totally absurd. No person can even begin to discern the hidden mysteries of God's creative purpose. Instead, Scripture everywhere celebrates the sheer incomparability of God: "To whom then will you liken God or what likeness compare with him? . . . Have you not known? Have you not heard? Has it not been told from the beginning? Have you not understood from the foundations of the earth? It is he who sits above the circle of the earth, and its inhabitants are like grasshoppers . . . who brings princes to naught, and makes the rulers of the earth as nothing" (Isa 40:18–23). The frail "powers" of earth's mightiest rulers are like stubble blown away by the tempest of God's incomparable majesty. God and God alone is *God*; the entire universe belongs to him and to him *alone*, not to us. For that reason, the church of Jesus Christ must reject as false doctrine the "dominion covenant" and the "creation mandate" of Christian Reconstructionism.

We proceed to a second point at issue. We hear from Christian Reconstructionism that the kingdom of God is a form of "Christian civilization"; that it was already begun by Christ, but is still to be "built" to completion by Christian political effort today. As was the case with the biblical exegesis of Rushdoony, we first need to point out that the overall structure of the authors' understanding of the kingdom of God is quite clearly a legacy of nineteenth-century Protestant liberalism, with its notion of the "progressive realization of the kingdom of God on earth" through human moral effort. The politics have changed—Hegelian idealism has been replaced by von Mises and Hayek—but the theological structure is identical. It is also worth remembering that the theological structure of nineteenth-century Protestant liberalism was utterly shattered by the publication in 1906 of Albert Schweitzer's classic study, *The Quest for the Historical Jesus*. In this book Schweitzer made it clear that the notion of the kingdom of God common among the nineteenth-century critics reflected the bourgeois culture of the time, not the New Testament. We can do no better than repeat Schweitzer's point, which applies equally to the ideas of the kingdom of God found in Christian Reconstructionism.

We ask: what is the Kingdom of God as proclaimed in the New Testament? One thing is certain: no one formula captures the complex mystery of the kingdom taught in the parables of Jesus. The kingdom of God is a gift; the initiative is with God and God alone. Yet it also comes as a demand to leave everything in order to inherit it. People receive it, inherit it, wait for it, enter it; they are challenged to seek it. No sacrifice is too costly in order to find it. It is hard for a wealthy person to enter it; only one who receives it like a child can come in. It is to be sought with one's entire being; the kingdom can in fact be taken away and given to another. The shrill excitement of the kingdom is prominent everywhere in New Testament proclamation. The kingdom is at hand; the long-expected time has now come; the new time of God's new world is even now breaking forth into reality as a divine event. The kingdom comes suddenly, so the right response is to watch, to be alert; the wrong response is go on with life as usual.

Now, the first point to be made is that, despite the enormous variety of formulation in the New Testament depiction of the mystery of the kingdom, one idea never used—not even once—is the notion of "building the kingdom of God." Inherit, receive, seek, wait, enter, even leave; never build. The notion was, as we have seen, a prominent feature of Protestant liberalism, and is now, in a very different political form, a prominent feature of Christian Reconstructionism. Yet, as Albert Schweitzer long ago made crystal clear, the idea has everything to say about the moral arrogance and self-righteousness of the times, and nothing at all to say about the teaching of the Bible. It is highly ironic that the very basis for conservative theological criticism of liberalism at the turn of the twentieth century—the notion that humankind can build God's kingdom on earth—is now a central feature of the latest manifestation of theological conservatism. Extremes meet. Both forms—liberal and conservative—fall far short of the witness of Scripture, and ultimately fall prey to the ancient heresy of Pelagianism, in which humanity and God "cooperate" together in working out the divine redemptive purpose. Only God builds his kingdom: "I planted, Apollos watered [aorist tense verbs: ministers come and go], but God gave the growth [imperfect tense verb: God alone continuously gives growth]" (1 Cor 3:6–7).

Furthermore, the biblical witness to the dialectical reality of God's time in the coming of the kingdom is essential. The standard liberal view—now picked up again by Christian Reconstructionism though converted to quite different political purposes—was that God's kingdom was *partially* fulfilled in the life and ministry of Jesus, but will only be *completely* fulfilled through human moral agency over progressive unfolding of time. Yet the contrast between the already and the not yet in the New Testament is of an entirely different order altogether. According to Mark (and the other Gospels agree in substance), the overall message of Jesus can be summarized: "The time is fulfilled, and the kingdom of God has come near; repent, and believe in the good news" (Mark 1:15). The kingdom of God is not partially here; it is *totally* here, right here and right now *completely* fulfilled. But it is now veiled, *hidden* in the secret of Christ's true identity as the suffering Messiah. Only the eyes of faith recognize that the kingdom has come in all its fullness in him. Others walk away disappointed: who can believe, they ask, that this carpenter's son from Nazareth hanging on the cross is God's Son? One day, however, it will be fully *manifest*, when the glory of the risen Christ will be universally visible. Not partial now, later complete; but hidden now, and only later fully manifest.

Now, it is essential to recognize that the Gospels leave the hiddenness of Christ's true identity intact, not just for the period of his earthly life (chronologically), but by the very nature of his true reality (ontologically). He is at the same time truly the Son of God, and yet hidden from unbelief. Christ's true identity is *only* known through his suffering and death; not only to the first generation of disciples, but to every new generation of the church. No one—not then, and not now—comes to the risen and glorified Christ, without first going the way of suffering and the cross. The hidden quality of Christ's true identity did not stop with the resurrection; it will stop only at his final appearing. Until then, the church follows Christ only in the shadow of the cross. Every form of Christian triumphalism—Christian Reconstructionism is just the latest in a long trend, sadly—is shattered by the offense of the gospel. At stake is what

Luther called the false theology of glory (*theologia gloriae*) versus the true theology of the cross (*theologia crucis*).

Perhaps most important of all in the New Testament understanding of the kingdom of God is simply this: Jesus Christ *is* the kingdom of God, and the kingdom of God *is* Jesus Christ. When Jesus says that the kingdom is among them (Luke 17:21), it is because *he* is among them. When Jesus says that the kingdom of God has come near (Mark 1:15), it is because *he* has come near, and is now in their very presence. As Origen long ago rightly observed, Jesus is the kingdom himself; the kingdom has come because he has come, and it will one day come again, because he, Christ the Lord, will come again. To pray: "thy kingdom come" in the New Testament is the same as to pray: "come, Lord Jesus." The confessing church therefore has a choice. We can either, with much pomp and circumstance, preach "Christian civilization" to the world, powerless and empty words with no substance; or we can in weakness and humility preach the true mystery of God's kingdom, which is the crucified and risen Lord Jesus Christ, effective in the power of God's almighty Spirit. Even to state the choice clearly is already to make it.

The third point at issue concerns the argument of the Christian Recontructionists for a new "evangelism through law." According to the Christian Reconstructionists, Christian "civilization" can win new converts to Christianity by enacting Christian moral legislation. Through following "Christian morality," the world will find Christ. Is this biblical? We have already offered a strong critique of the moral legalism of Rushdoony. We argued that, at stake in the rejection of Christian Reconstructionism, is the fundamental Pauline formulation of justification by grace through faith, apart from all works of the law. The idea of a new "evangelism through law" not only forces us to raise the issue again, but to carry our critique even further.

Throughout his epistles, but especially in his letters to the Romans and the Galatians, Paul drives home the point again and again that the gospel and the gospel alone—not the law—is the divine gift of redeeming love for the world. The theme of the entire epistle to the Romans is sounded forth in the opening verses: "For I am not ashamed of the gospel: it is the power of God for salvation to everyone who has faith, to the Jew first and also to the Greek. For in it the righteousness of God is revealed through faith for faith . . ." (Rom 1:16–17). Being put right with God comes not through works of the law as a human achievement, but through the free gift of God's grace in Jesus Christ: "in Christ, God was reconciling the world to himself, not counting their trespasses against them, and entrusting the message of reconciliation to us" (2 Cor 5:19). Thus, the message of reconciliation to God that the church offers to the world is the forgiveness of sins through God's free justification of the ungodly: "But to one who without works trusts him who justifies the ungodly, such faith is reckoned as righteousness" (Rom 4:5). Christ did not come to the morally accomplished, but to the morally bankrupt: "For while we were still weak, at the right time Christ died for the ungodly . . . God proves his love for us in that while we still were sinners Christ died for us" (Rom 6:6–8). God's power alone accomplishes our justification, which in no sense whatsoever can be ascribed to human moral effort: "yet we know that a person is justified not by the works of the law but through faith in Jesus Christ. And we have come to believe in Christ Jesus, so that we might be justified by faith in Christ, and not by doing the works of the law, because no one will be justified by the works of the law" (Gal 2:16). Faith and works, according to Paul, are *total opposites*; there can be no human cooperation in salvation, which comes to the world as a sheer gift of divine mercy alone. Paul hammers home the point without ambiguity: the righteousness of God (God's saving covenant love for the world) has been revealed "apart from the law." And this is no new doctrine according to Paul; this is the same doctrine attested by "all the law and the prophets" (Rom 3:21). We are not justified before God through any intrinsic moral worth, but solely through the imputation of Christ's own righteousness: "Therefore his faith was reckoned to him as righteousness . . . it will be reckoned to us who believe in him who raised Jesus our Lord from the dead" (Rom 4:23–24). Those who have received the divine gift of acquittal are rendered a new creation by the presence of the Spirit: "So if anyone is in Christ, there is a new creation: everything old has passed away; see, everything has become new!" (2 Cor 5:17). Declaration of forgiveness (justification) and newness of life (sanctification) must always be distinguished; but they cannot be separated.

Now, before we proceed further, I think it is worth pausing a moment to gain some historical context. Some misunderstandings of the biblical message are repeated sufficiently often that they are ontological in nature; that is, they are *always there* waiting for fresh adherents to open the door once again. Such is the threat of moralistic legalism, which time and again has tempted the church, just as it is now in the form of Christian

Reconstrucionism. The temptation is not new. For example, in the later Middle Ages a movement arose known to scholars as medieval nominalism. According to late medieval nominalism, as long as a person does the best they can (*facere quod in se est*), God will not deny them grace. That is, human persons are able to love God as the law requires according to their own natural ability, even if that love is imperfect (*meritum de congruo*). It was this medieval version of "evangelism by law" that the Protestant Reformers rejected so decisively by their doctrine of "by faith alone." And not only the Reformers: Thomas Aquinas had already insisted that grace is absolutely prior to human acts of free will, and therefore no human being is able on their own strength to prepare oneself to receive divine salvation. According to Thomas we do not initiate faith, God alone does. Faith begins, only when grace comes. There is no talk of "doing the best you can" as a way to salvation in Thomas Aquinas: "If a man does what he can, people say, God will not deny him grace. Yes, but a man can do whatever God *moves* him to do. . . . Man prepares himself by his own free will, but not without help from God *activating* him and drawing him to himself [italics mine]."[4] By sharp contrast to Thomas and the Reformers, Christian Reconstructionism would write yet a new chapter in the long history of neo-Pelagian moralism, offering the world access to Christ through moral achievement based on works of the law. We must follow the mainstream of the church through time and answer once again: no.

Why was the issue so absolutely either/or for Paul? And why did Augustine, Thomas, Luther, Calvin, and confessional Christianity at large affirm Paul with the decisiveness of this issue? Is it simply a matter of two theological principles at stake, the principle of justification versus the principle of law? If so, why not forge some sort of compromise? Why not join the two principles into an even higher theological principle embracing both? These are fair questions, and they deserve a clear, biblically-based answer.

The fact is, the doctrine of justification by grace through faith is not a principle; it is a true and necessary implication of the atoning death of Jesus Christ for the sins of the world. Paul insists on justification apart from all works of the law because the full reality of Christ's atoning death demands it. Paul directly connects justification and atonement: "For there is no distinction, since all have sinned and fall short of the glory of God;

---

4. Thomas Aquinas, *Summa Theologiae*, 310.

they are now justified by his grace as a gift, through the redemption that is in Christ Jesus, whom God put forward as a sacrifice of atonement by his blood, effective through faith" (Rom 3:22–25). Justification is a gift of God, not on the basis of a general idea of divine benevolence, but solely on the grounds of the cross of Jesus Christ. God is the one who offers the atoning sacrifice, not the one who is "propitiated"; God does not need to be reconciled to the world, the world needs to be reconciled to God. But nor is Christ's death a mere *example* of divine love (as in Protestant liberalism); rather, it is through the atonement accomplished on the cross that human sin is covered, for our sake, and indeed in our place. Romans 4:25 makes the connection between justification and atonement firm and clear: "(Christ) was handed over to death for our trespasses and was raised for our justification." Our guilt before God is objective and real (not a "guilty conscience"). The cross of Christ is the one event of God's love where that guilt is removed, not as a punishment offered to God, but as a liberation from the power and guilt of sin. That is why, for Paul, absolutely *everything* rests on justification by grace alone; for behind justification stands the cross, and there is no truth behind, before, above, or after the cross worth knowing at all.

Why then did the early church reject Pelagianism? Why did Thomas, Luther, and Calvin reject the medieval version of semi-Pelagianism? And why must we reject the neo-Pelagianism of Christian Reconstructionism? Why is "evangelism through law" not only wrong as a "technique," but a profound distortion of the gospel? The answer in all cases is the same: because Jesus Christ died for the sins of the world, and our only hope is in him. We preach Christ and him crucified; that is the only evangelism of the confessing church, now and forever.

We come now to our final point of critical response to North and DeMar; and in fact it can stand as our final criticism of the set of ideas which make up Christian Reconstructionism as a whole. According to the Reconstructionists, Christians are called to *dominion* over the world, through the spread of "Christian civilization." Indeed, the set of ideas is often called "dominion theology" for just this reason. Is this biblical? Is this Christian? We are not here addressing insignificant matters of doctrine, but probing at the very heart of what it means to be a follower of Jesus Christ in our world today. No issue could be more crucial for the life of the church.

We begin with a passage from Mark (though it is reproduced in similar form in Matthew and Luke as well). Jesus tells the disciples that he *must* endure great suffering, be rejected by the religious authorities, and be killed; and after three days rise again. He is not making a prediction; he is declaring a truth grounded in divine necessity which lies beyond the human ability to comprehend. Luke's Gospel in particular stresses that the whole life of Jesus moves forward in suffering under this same divine *must*, this same divine necessity. Peter of course rejects the idea entirely. Perhaps a suffering Messiah is acceptable, he allows, but only in the form of a magnificent and celebrated martyrdom; certainly not after being rejected by the established religious authorities! Jesus immediately dismisses Peter's objection as a temptation to veer away from the genuine path of obedience; the divine *must* outweighs every other consideration. We come to our text: "If any want to become my followers, let them deny themselves and take up their cross and follow me. For those who want to save their life will lose it, and those who lose their life for my sake, and for the sake of the gospel, will save it" (Mark 10:34–35). There is thus an insoluble link between the suffering of Christ and the form of Christian life. To live for Jesus Christ is to share in the cross which he himself necessarily endured. Denying oneself is not here simply a matter of putting away sin; it is a matter of putting away self as the center of existence. It is a moment of radical decision (the aorist tense); yet in Luke it is also a taking up of one's cross daily in a repeated process. The point is: bearing the cross is not a trivial exercise in "spirituality" or "piety"; it is to leave everything behind, all that we have and all that we are. Yet self-denial is not an end in itself; the purpose is so as to follow Jesus Christ, that is, to be his disciple. Here, the tense of the verb suggests a continuous relationship, not just a once-for-all decision; following Christ is for a lifetime, a new orientation of one's entire being, not a matter of isolated acts. A choice has to be made: the disciple who tries to save his or her life by denying Christ, will lose the only life that really matters: eternal life with him. The disciple who loses his or her life for his sake, will gain the greatest treasure. Mark adds that it is for the sake of the gospel, the good news; discipleship costs everything, but the cost is embraced, not with resignation, but in exhilaration and joy. Mark almost certainly means this form of discipleship literally: actual martyrdom for the sake of Christian confession. But in the larger context of the biblical canon, the call to discipleship has been rendered at a metaphorical level; to live for Christ is to leave everything behind, and to follow him alone. Luke 14:27 summarizes the whole point: "Whoever does not carry the cross cannot be my disciple." To be a Christian is to suffer for the sake of Christ.

Where, we ask, is the *slightest hint* of a call to "dominion? Where does Jesus say: "if you would follow me, you must rule over everything, just as I do"? What is at stake is not a controversial debate over certain issues of Christian ethics; what is at stake is nothing less than the basic form of Christian life itself. Christ suffered on the cross by a divine necessity; the cruciform nature of Christian existence is established by that same necessity. To know Christ is to share in the suffering of the cross; not to *imitate* him, but to *participate* in his suffering. To find "dominion" in the world is to lose the cross.

A second passage drives the point home with inescapable clarity. Jesus is speaking to the disciples: "You know that among the Gentiles those whom they recognize as their rulers lord it over them, and their great ones are tyrants over them. But it is not so among you; but whoever wishes to become great among you must be your servant, and whoever wishes to be first among you must be slave of all. For the Son of Man came not to be served but to serve, and to give his life a ransom for many" (Mark 10:42–45). The background is a discussion among the disciples about which of them will rise to the top in the coming kingdom of God. Who will rule next to Christ? As Calvin points out, the disciples still have yet to learn the whole point of Christian discipleship. Jesus counters with an unforgettable reversal of their understanding. In the surrounding culture, those who are recognized as rulers have great power and authority over others. There is concealed irony here; they are "recognized" as rulers, but of course God alone is the real ruler. In the surrounding world of culture, to be great, and to exercise dominion, are equated; they are the same thing. By sharp contrast, in the new world of God, the equation is turned upside down. In God's new world, to be truly great is to be a servant; to render personal service to others. The culture of the time values "dominion" and despises the lowly "servant," but in God's new world dominion is overturned, and the servant is rendered truly worthy. All worldly ideas of status, rank, and privilege are totally foreign to God's new world, where God chooses those who are "nothing" in this world to shame those who are "something" (1 Cor 1:26–31). The call to service is not a moral principle or value; it is rather a concrete commandment grounded in the mission of Christ himself, who gave his life for the world.

Unlike the rulers of this world, Christ the Lord of all served, he was not served; to follow him is to bear his life of service to others.

We ask: where does Christ ever call his disciples to "dominion" over the world? In fact, he *warns* them not to fall into the trap of imitating the way of the world, which is precisely the form of "dominion." Dominion is actually the ultimate weakness; for it only remains strong as long as it can show itself strong to the world around, and that is no strength at all. We are called by Christ to *service*, not dominion. Service is the true strength. As Gregory of Nyssa brilliantly argues, any form of power can act "power-fully"; that is, according to its nature. But only God's power is so great that it can take the form of a servant, without being any less divine: "It does not startle us to hear it said that the whole creation, including the invisible world, exists by God's power, and is the realization of his will. But descent to man's lowly position is a supreme example of power—of a power which is not bounded by circumstances contrary to its nature."[5] God is so powerful, that unlike the pitiful kings of the earth—who can only do what pitiful kings have always done—he alone can become a servant, without being any less divine. The way of the world, which is dominion, or the way of Christ, which is service; these are not two equally interesting options. These constitute a choice, a basic decision, over which rests the life or death of the church. In his service alone lies perfect freedom.

---

5. Gregory of Nyssa, *Address on Religious Instruction,* 300. (This text is perhaps more familiarly known as *Catechetical Oration.*)

Epilogue

WE HAVE BEEN COMPELLED by the nature of the case to answer Christian Reconstructionism with a definitive No. Our argument has been that, given the various views clearly presented by the authors in prominent texts, the primary set of ideas which form the substance of Christian Reconstructionism fall well outside the legitimate boundaries of Christian confession as defined by the norm of Holy Scripture, and as recognized by the historic mainstream church. However, if we must say no, it can only be for one reason: in order all the more clearly to speak God's Yes to the world through Jesus Christ.

We cannot offer here an alternative social ethics; to do so would turn a brief theological response into an elaborate systematic treatise. We can, however, at least offer four theological ideas of our own for thoughtful reflection and meditation: wisdom, freedom, solidarity, and fairness. Even if in this small way, it is crucial to stress that God's Yes has already won the victory.

The standpoint of our four ideas will be quite different from Christian Reconstructionism, for several reasons. First of all, Christian Reconstructionism is by definition backward looking. It seeks to reconstruct something from the past—and that is the creation mandate of the Garden of Eden. By contrast, the Bible is *always forward looking*. Abraham is called to leave his native land, and promised a new homeland. Moses and the Israelites are delivered from bondage in Egypt, and brought out to a new land "flowing with milk and honey." The ultimate hope of the prophets is a new creation of earth and heaven. Nor does the New Testament end this forward looking stance, as if the fulfillment of the promise in Christ empties hope of all content. Not at all: "For in hope we were saved. Now hope that is seen is not hope. For who hopes for what is seen? But if we hope for what we do not see, we wait for it with patience" (Rom 8:24–25). Nowhere—not once—does the Bible speak of salvation in terms of a return to paradise (*restitutio in integrum*), which is a pagan myth. The Bible always points forward to the coming Day of Jesus Christ, who is the one hope of all the earth. We are saved by hope, not by nostalgia: "Do not say, 'Why were the former days better than these?' For it is not from wisdom that you ask this" (Eccl 7:10).

Secondly, we must recognize the ethical pattern of the indicative and the imperative in the Bible, which Christian Reconstructionism routinely reverses. Reconstructionism says: first build God's kingdom on earth (the imperative), then the kingdom of Christ will be universal (the indicative). The Bible—and a biblically based social ethics—moves in the opposite direction. The Bible says, Christ already is the ruler of the heavens and the earth; all things already belong to him; nothing hinders his will, which encompasses the entire cosmos (the indicative). Therefore, leave everything behind, and follow me (the imperative). The gift of the kingdom always *precedes* the demand which it brings. Jesus Christ, who *is* the kingdom of God, is present now among us; that is why we are called to a radically new way of life.

Thirdly, we must resist the temptation to replace one -ism (Christian Reconstruction-ism) with yet another -ism. The church is surely tired of a politicized gospel, whether it comes from the religious left or the religious right; tired of political ideologies looking to Christianity and the Bible for *confirmation* of their view, rather than fresh *discovery* of the truth. When it comes to social ethics, the Bible resists all causes; its only concern is the real life needs of concrete people. The Parable of the Good Samaritan is the classic test. A man lay dying by the side of the road, beaten and robbed. The priest and the Levite go out of their way to avoid him; they see only the abstract moral cause to which they are committed, and fail even to *see* the sheer reality of a suffering fellow human being. Only the Samaritan—a foreigner, a heretic—sees the concrete reality of human need, and proves to be a genuine neighbor. The gospel makes *invisible* humanity visible.

God has already transformed the entire universe through the death and resurrection of Jesus Christ. God's new world is already a reality. The community of faith is called together as a new humanity, a visible sign in the world of God's gracious purpose for the whole creation. Christian social ethics therefore means sharing in a *new society*. What shape does that new society take?

We begin with the relation of Christian faith to culture. How is the Christian community in the world today to relate to human culture in the broadest sense? Three broad answers present themselves. The church can simply *accept* the surrounding culture as an absolute, seeking to redefine its message with reference to the criteria of meaning and truth found there. This was the answer made famous in the prolegomena to Schleiermacher's *The Christian Faith* and can only lead, in my judgment, into the self-dissolving doctrinal indifferentism of neo-Protestantism. Again, the church can simply *reject* culture, defining itself in dualistic opposition to culture as evil. This is certainly the answer of Christian Reconstructionism, and as we have seen, runs up against the dialectical form of Scripture itself, which resists all easy dualism. The third approach—which I believe represents the best insights of the mainstream Christian community through time, as well as the present—is more subtle, and in the end more fruitful. On the one hand, God's new world is already here in the gospel of Jesus Christ who rules all things. We belong to him alone; the moral values of human culture are overturned by his glorious rule. On the other hand, we continue to serve Christ in the old world which is passing away. Already transferred to the new, yet still living out our life in the old. And here we find the stunning surprise: God has not given up on his world. Despite the Fall, God maintains all humanity in his image; and in his image, excellence is found in the most unusual places. Culture (art, science, literature, music, etc.) is not an absolute good, nor is it an absolute evil; at its best moments, it can be a *relative good* from which the Christian can derive a measure of truth and insight in the journey of faith.

The intersection of the *already* and the *not yet* takes place in what the Bible calls *wisdom*. The personified figure of wisdom in the Bible is a public figure, a cultural figure, summoning the human community at large: "Does not wisdom call, and does not understanding raise her voice? On the heights, beside the way, at the crossroads she takes her stand . . . to you, O people, I call . . . acquire intelligence, you who lack it" (Prov 8:1–5). To know wisdom is to gain insight into the world, and how it works; to learn to communicate but also to listen effectively. Wisdom gains understanding of science, technology, medicine, economics; simply because they are part of our world, and therefore part of God's world. Wisdom learns beauty; not the false beauty of the merely glamorous, but the true beauty of protest and hidden affirmation. Wisdom learns why people do what they do, not the surface motives loudly announced, but the hidden motives usually carefully concealed. Wisdom works hard to change what can be changed; it sometimes learns the hard way to cut its losses when real change is, for the time being, impossible. Wisdom finds joy where it is truly found: in the fulfillment of hard work, in the pleasures of gentle rest, in the glories of true friendship, in the ecstasy of satisfied love. Wisdom always discerns right from wrong; but it also sees the gray areas of life where compromise is what is required, where finding common ground through consensus is the only wise course to take. Wisdom is willing to make an acceptable compromise rather than achieve a decisive victory if the common good requires it. Wisdom tells me that pride and strength are a mere appearance; that gentleness and humility are at the core of human existence. Wisdom constantly whispers in my ear that the truly wealthy in this world are those who have what they need, no matter how little that might be; and ultimate blessing comes not from the having, but from the giving away.

The world of culture is *not* the Word of God; but nor is it the word of the devil. The world of culture is a human and humane voice to which the wise Christian is always open, always ready to listen, always eager to learn.

We proceed to a second major theme of our theological response to Christian Reconstructionism: the separation of church and state. What should the attitude of the confessing church of Jesus Christ in our time be, to the separation of church and state, based on the authoritative witness of Holy Scripture? Before answering directly, we need to demythologize the Christian home-school "textbook" version of early American history now circulating among Christian Reconstructionists. Its thesis runs something like this: "Europe was an evil, secular place, so the early Puritans came to America to establish a national church, a Christian state. The first Amendment—guaranteeing religious freedom—was never meant to apply to the states; therefore, the idea of a state church is still constitutional. The current threat to that state church is coming from the new secular humanism, the same humanism once found in the old world." This is being taught as "history." Now, I have no intention of rehearsing early American history in a work such as the present one; readers can find an authoritative summary in the excellent account by Mark A. Noll, *America's God*. However, the homeschool myth needs to be exposed for what it is: a piece of political propaganda, not an historical account. The fact is, the Europe that the early Puritans left was a place in which the national church was the *norm*. They came to America to *escape* the national church, not to *establish* it. The first amendment, forbidding the establishment of a national church, and guaranteeing the freedom of religion, was not a *threat* to the confessing faith of the church of Jesus Christ, but rather a genuine *expression* of exactly why the original religious dissenters and exiles came here in the first place. Nor is the first amendment *now* under threat from "secular humanism"; if it is under threat at all, it is under threat from the misguided zeal of Christian Reconstructionists, who would trade our freedom for a new bondage to the old *European* ideal of a national church.

The issue is not simply historical accuracy, but theological confession. As the community of faith in Jesus Christ we affirm religious freedom, expressed in the separation of church and state. Our freedom as Christians, however, does *not* come from the first amendment of the Constitution, or from any human document; our freedom comes as a gift from God, and from God alone. We are free to proclaim Jesus Christ in word and deed, whether we live in a democracy, or under the worst tyranny. Paul himself, writing from jail in chains, still maintains with magisterial freedom: "But the word of God is not chained" (2 Tim 2:9). God alone is our true freedom. Yet precisely because of God's gift of freedom, we as Christians affirm the inherent good of democracy for all peoples; and we furthermore believe that no democracy is genuine unless it gives religious freedom to all citizens. As followers of Christ we reject a totalitarian state which seeks to control the affairs of the church; as followers of Christ we just as readily reject a totalitarian church which seeks to control the affairs of the state. A Christianity which aims at "political influence" and ultimately at "a Christian state" will finally become nothing more than an arm of the state, and at that very moment cease to be the church of Jesus Christ.

What are the theological issues at stake in our affirmation of religious freedom? First of all, the fundamental divine claim upon our existence is at stake: God is holy; we are therefore called to be holy unto him. We are *God's own people*; our primary citizenship is in his realm. The idea of a "Christian state" puts an earthly king in the place of God himself, which is ultimate disaster: "Do not put your trust in princes, in mortals, in whom there is no help. When their breath departs, they return to the earth; on that very day their plans perish" (Ps 146:3–4). As the community of faith in Jesus Christ we believe in the separation of church and state, not as a *concession* to the state, but as an *affirmation* of the holiness of God.

Second of all, we believe in the Ten Commandments as the law of our life together, which is the law of love. To find life and joy is to do God's commandments. Yet we have no interest whatsoever in converting the Ten Commandments into human legislation, for one simple reason: the Ten Commandments are the *Law of Christ*, and he alone is their one true Interpreter. Christ alone interprets God's law for the world; to place that law into the hands of human government is to profane the holy: "Do not give what is holy to dogs; and do not throw your pearls before swine, or they will trample them under foot . . ." (Matt 7:6). And thirdly, the church does not engage the world by moralistic legislation—that way lies nothing but the secularization of the church itself. We offer the world a light more powerful than any human laws ever written.

Our third major theme arises from the new global reality of the Christian community. The era of Western Christian dominance is now at an end; the advent of a new global Christianity is here, and here to stay. We are, in my opinion, in an exactly analogous situation to the New Testament church when God's Word and Spirit first came to the Gentiles. Will the Gentiles—the nations—be forced to embrace mosaic legislation in order to become Christians? At the apostolic council (Acts 15), the church answered with a definitive no; Gentile Christians are free to serve the risen Lord—as Gentiles. The question in our time is equally basic: do Christians in Africa, Latin America, Asia, etc., first need to embrace Western culture in order to be Christian? The same answer must surely be given: no, Africans serve the risen Lord as Africans, not as Westernized Christians. The issue at stake is basic to biblical theology. God's Word and Spirit are not mediated through Western culture, or through any one form of the institutional church; "the wind blows where it chooses" (John 3:8). The Spirit—not Western culture—is the church's link with the risen Christ through the medium of the proclaimed word; and that word freely addresses every indigenous culture in its own idiom. The mere fact of Bible translation is an indirect conformation of the freedom of God's Word and Spirit to speak in new ways to new peoples. Lamin Sanneh wisely points out: "Bible translation was a shelter for indigenous ideas and values."[1]

Now, there is a unity in the brilliant diversity of global Christianity. That unity is not exported Western culture or Westernized Christianity, but something far more profound. The unity within the diversity of the

---

1. Sanneh, *Whose Religion*, 109.

global church is first of all *Jesus Christ* himself. We are God's building, but the one foundation of that building is Christ: "For no one can lay any foundation other than the one that has been laid; that foundation is Jesus Christ" (1 Cor 3:11). Christ alone is the true unity of the church, who gathers all his children in all lands and nations together into one. Second of all, there is a *pattern of truth* binding all Christians in all cultures into one. That pattern is not *Western*; that pattern is *biblical*. Each in our own way, Christians in all cultures discern the shape of Christian truth attested in Scripture. Whether the content of that pattern is articulated in Korea, Madagascar, Togo, Brazil, Cuba, Chile, Indonesia, or countless other places where Christ is served, the shape is evident (the reader is invited to peruse the excellent collection of confessions by the global church included in volume three of Pelikan, *Creeds and Confessions of Faith in the Christian Tradition*, cited in the bibliography). And thirdly, there is a *pattern of life*—giving shape to the way of discipleship—similarly evident in the language of faith and action spoken throughout the global Christian community. Unity is not uniformity; legitimate diversity remains, as the fourfold Gospel itself exemplifies. Yet the diversity is upheld in unity: for we worship one Lord, are filled with one Spirit, and together serve one God.

The new global reality of Christians radically changes the way we as Christians see the world around us. Human beings draw circles of acceptance; those on the inside are worthy, those on the outside are unworthy. Nations draw borders; classes draw social distinctions; tribes draw boundaries. The God of the Bible seems to take supreme pleasure in crossing the boundaries drawn by human beings. He crosses national borders, bringing healing to Namaan the Syrian general (2 Kings 5). He overturns social distinctions, rescuing Rahab the prostitute of Jericho (Josh 6). He ignores the "inner circle" of religion, embracing Ruth the Moabite, great-grandmother of David the great King. Now, there is nothing wrong with being a *patriot*; a patriot affirms national greatness in all its splendor. A *nationalist,* by sharp contrast, believes that such greatness grants a right to impose national will upon others. As global Christians in a global society, we condemn nationalism in all its forms. We recognize our solidarity with our fellow humanity among all peoples, in all nations of the earth.

We conclude by considering the issue of state obligation to care for the poor. Christian Reconstructionism systematically denies that the state has *any* obligation to the poor; indeed any obligation to the general welfare of its citizens overall. Care for the poor is assigned solely to families and churches. Is this biblical? In an era when the income gap between wealthy and poor is only growing greater, the question is hardly insignificant. We will proceed along two levels of reflection.

Our first answer is simply to point out that the Bible does in fact assign care of the poor to the state, without any ambiguity. Psalm 72, perhaps written by David for Solomon to describe the duties of the ideal king, stresses obligation to the poor: "May he defend the cause of the poor of the people, give deliverance to the needy and crush the oppressor . . . For he delivers the needy when they call, the poor and those who have no helper. He has pity on the weak and the needy, and saves the lives of the needy. From oppression and violence he redeems their life; and precious is their blood in his sight" (Ps 72:4, 12–14). This is not describing a family, or the church; this is a clear mandate to *state* obligation for the poor in a description of the *ideal* government. Again, the book of Proverbs likewise describes the duties of the ideal king in very similar terms: "Speak out for those who cannot speak, for the rights of the destitute. Speak out, judge righteously, defend the rights of the poor and needy" (Prov 31:8–9). It is precisely the role of the king to give voice to the voiceless in society. Similarly, in the law of Moses, it is the role of the courts to protect the rights of the poor: "You shall not pervert the justice due to your poor in their lawsuits . . . You shall not oppress a resident alien; you know the heart of an alien, for you were aliens in the land of Egypt" (Exod 23:6–9). And of course the prophets of the Old Testament never tire of launching attack after attack against the kings of Israel and Judah for their complacent lack of care for the needy: "Listen, you heads of Jacob and rulers of the house of Israel! Should you not know justice?—you who hate the good and love the evil, who tear the skin off my people, and the flesh off their bones . . . Hear this, you rulers of the house of Jacob and chiefs of the house of Israel, who abhor justice and pervert all equity . . . because of you Zion shall be plowed up" (Mic 3: 1–3, 9–12). On the first level, our answer to the question before us is a straightforward and simple yes: the Bible most certainly assigns care of the poor and needy to the state. Denial of this fact by Christian Reconstructionism certainly has nothing to do with the Bible or Christian doctrine based upon it, but comes rather from a political ideology foreign to the message of Scripture.

But here we need, in closing, to dig to a deeper, more profound level. Jesus describes a final judgment in which all nations—not families, not churches, but *nations*, including their governments—will be gathered before him (Matt 25:31–46). Notice, by the way, that the much vaunted issue of national exceptionalism is a divine prerogative, not a human one; only Christ alone has the right to decide which nations are truly exceptional. How will he decide? He makes it crystal clear in this passage. Care for the poor is not *an* obligation of the state; it is in some sense *the* obligation of the state. Nations will not be judged by whether they have a powerful military; nor whether they have a strong middle class. Nations—all nations—will be judged, not by a fallible human judgment, but by the only judgment that really matters, by the Lord of all nations—on one basis only: how did you care for the weak and the needy? Did you feed the hungry among you, or let them struggle to survive? Did you give the thirsty something to drink, or watch callously as they scrambled for every scrap? Do you provide for the health and well-being of the sick and the dying, or force them to choose between the medication they need and food to keep alive? Did you welcome the stranger to your shores, or with hardness of heart build walls to keep them away? Did you treat even the prisoners among you with the humanity they still retain, despite their mistakes in life? Did you provide clothing to the naked, or turn away from what is "no concern of mine"? This is not a question of "social policy." Christ makes it all too clear that far more is at stake. How nations—including their governments—treat the poor, is how they treat Christ himself: "Truly I tell you, just as you did not do it to one of the least of these, you did not do it to me" (Matt 25:45). This is not capitalism, or socialism, or any other -ism; this is the Word of the Lord; thanks be to God . . .

Bibliography

Augustine, *On Christian Doctrine*. Translated by D. W. Robertson. New York: Bobbs-Merrill, 1958.

Bavinck, H. *Synopsis Purioris Theologiae*. Leiden: Didericum Donner, 1881.

Butler, Joseph. *The Analogy of Religion*. New York: Ungar, 1961.

Calvin, John. *A Harmony of the Gospels*. In *Calvin's New Testament Commentaries*, volumes 1–3. Grand Rapids: Eerdmans, 1975.

———. *Commentaries on the Book of Genesis*. Translated by Rev. John King. Grand Rapids: Baker, 1979.

———. *Institutes of the Christian Religion*. Translated by Ford Lewis Battles. Philadelphia: Westminster, 1960.

Diamond, Sara. *Roads to Dominion*. New York: Guilford, 1995.

Flacius, Matthias. *De Ratione Cognoscendi Sacras Literas*. Dusseldorf: Stern Verlag, 1968.

Frei, Hans. *The Eclipse of Biblical Narrative*. New Haven: Yale University Press, 1974.

Gaither, Milton. *Homeschool: An American History*. New York: Macmillan, 2008.

Gerhard, Johann. *Loci Theologici*. Leipzig: Hinrichs, 1885.

Gregory of Nyssa. *Address on Religious Instruction*. In *Library of Christian Classics*, volume 3. Philadelphia: Westminster, 1964.

Irenaeus. *Against All Heresies*. In *Ante-Nicene Fathers*, volume 1. Grand Rapids: Eerdmans, 1996.

Jacobsen, Douglas. *The World's Christians*. Oxford: Blackwell, 2011.

Kuyper, Abraham. *Encyclopedia of Sacred Theology*. Translated by Hendrik de Vries. New York: Scribners, 1898.

Lienesch, Michael. *Redeeming America*. Chapel Hill: University of North Carolina Press, 1993.

Lohse, Bernhard. *Martin Luther's Theology*. Translated by Roy Harrisville. Minneapolis: Fortress, 1999.

Luther, Martin. *Lectures on Galatians*. In *Luther's Works*, volumes 26–27. St Louis: Concordia, 1963.

———. *How Christians Should Regard Moses*. In *Luther's Works*, volume 35. Philadelphia: Muhlenberg, 1960.

———. *Preface to Epistle of St. Paul to the Romans*. In *Luther's Works*, volume 35. Philadelphia: Muhlenberg, 1960.

———. *Lectures on Romans*. In *Luther's Works*, volume 25. St Louis: Concordia, 1972.

Marckius, Johannes. *Christianae Theologiae Medulla*. Philadelphia: Anderson, 1824.

Marsden, George. *Fundamentalism and American Culture.* Oxford: Oxford University Press, 2006.

Noll, Mark. *America's God.* Oxford: Oxford University Press, 2002.

North, Gary, and Gary DeMar. *Christian Reconstructionism.* Tyler, TX: Institute for Christian Economics, 1991.

Pelikan, Jaroslav, and Valerie Hotschkiss. *Creeds and Confessions of Faith in the Christian Tradition.* 3 volumes. New Haven: Yale University Press, 2003.

Polanus, Amandus. *Syntagma Theologiae Christianae.* Hanover: 1610.

Rauschenbusch, Walter. *A Theology for the Social Gospel.* New York: MacMillan, 1917.

Ritschl, Albrecht. *Three Essays.* Translated by Philip Hefner. Philadelphia: Fortress, 1972.

Rushdoony, Rousas John. *The Institutes of Biblical Law.* Nutley, NJ: The Craig Press, 1973.

Sanneh, Lamin. *Whose Religion is It?* Grand Rapids: Eerdmans, 2003.

Schaeffer, Francis. *A Christian Manifesto.* Wheaton, IL: Crossway, 1981.

Tertullian. *The Prescription Against Heretics.* In *Ante-Nicene Fathers,* volume 3. Grand Rapids: Eerdmans, 1997.

Thomas Aquinas, *Summa Theologiae: A Concise Translation.* Edited by Timothy McDermott. Allen, TX: Christian Classics, 1989.

Turrettin, Francis. *Institutio Theologiae Elencticae.* Trajecti ad Rhenum, 1734.

Ursinus, Zacharias. *Commentary on the Heidelberg Catechism.* Phillipsburg: Presbyterian and Reformed Publishing, n.d.

Van Til, Cornelius. *A Christian Theory of Knowledge.* Grand Rapids: Baker, 1969.

Ware, Kallistos. *The Orthodox Church.* Harmondsworth: Penguin, 1975.

Wollebius, Johannes. *Compendium Theologiae Christianae.* In *Reformed Dogmatics.* Translated by John Beardslee III. New York: Oxford University Press, 1965.

Printed in Japan
落丁、乱丁本のお問い合わせは
Amazon.co.jp カスタマーサービスへ

6447413R00083